Ethical Standards
in Social Work

Ethical Standards
in Social Work

A REVIEW OF THE *NASW CODE OF ETHICS*

2ND EDITION

FREDERIC G. REAMER

NASW PRESS

NATIONAL ASSOCIATION OF SOCIAL WORKERS
WASHINGTON, DC

Elvira Craig de Silva, DSW, ACSW, President
Elizabeth J. Clark, PhD, ACSW, MPH, Executive Director

Cheryl Y. Bradley, Publisher
Schandale Kornegay, Executive Editor
Marcia D. Roman, Managing Editor, Journals and Books
Kathie P. Baker, Editor
Christina A. Davis, Copy Editor
Rebecca W. Tippets, Proofreader
Bernice Eisen, Indexer

Cover design by Anne Masters, Anne Masters Design Inc.
Interior design by Circle Graphics
Printed and bound by Port City Press, Baltimore, MD

Library of Congress Cataloging-in-Publication Data

Reamer, Frederic G., 1953-
   Ethical standards in social work : a review of the NASW code of
ethics / by Frederic G. Reamer.
      p. cm.
   Includes bibliographical references and index.
   ISBN 13 978-0-87101-371-1
   ISBN 0-87101-371-1
   1. Social workers—Professional ethics—United States. 2. National
Association of Social Workers. Code of ethics of the National
Association of Social Workers.   I. Title.
   HV40.8.U6R43 2006
   174'.9362—dc22
                                                      2006002616

For
Deborah, Emma, and *Leah*

Special dedication to
Elizabeth DuMez and *Charles Levy,*
true champions of social work ethics

Contents

Preface

Ethical standards in social work have been transformed. Like all other professionals, in recent years, social workers' understanding of ethical issues has matured dramatically. When the National Association of Social Workers (NASW) published its first code of ethics in 1960, the entire set of 14 guidelines fit on one side of one page. The current *Code*—ratified by the NASW Delegate Assembly in 1996, implemented in 1997, and revised modestly in 1999—comprises 155 ethical standards and six broad ethical principles. In the time between, social workers have developed an enriched grasp of the profession's core values, the ways in which core values sometimes conflict in practice, and ethical dilemmas in the profession. In addition, social workers have become more familiar with patterns of ethical misconduct engaged in by a relatively small portion of the profession's members.

The *NASW Code of Ethics*, which constitutes a marked change in the profession's understanding of and approach to ethical issues, reflects this remarkable transformation. It embodies what we have learned about ethics throughout social work's history—most of which has emerged since 1980, when the broader field of applied and professional ethics began to burgeon.

This book has several purposes. First, it provides social workers with a detailed overview and discussion of the *NASW Code of Ethics*. It includes a summary of the evolution of ethical issues in the profession; discussion of the profession's core values, mission, and broad ethical principles; and explanations and illustrations of the profession's more specific ethical standards. My hope is that the material will provide the profession with a useful educational tool for use by both experienced and fledgling practitioners.

In addition, this book should be useful to social workers who seek advice and consultation on ethical issues. Although *Ethical Standards in Social Work* cannot provide formulaic solutions to all ethical issues and should be supplemented by other literature and resources pertaining to social work and professional ethics, it can provide social workers with an overview of relevant guidelines and issues as they sort their way through ethical thickets.

Ethical Standards in Social Work should also be useful to social workers and others who rely on the *NASW Code of Ethics* in relation to ethics complaints and lawsuits involving social workers. Members of NASW ethics committees and state licensing boards, and those engaged in litigation involving social workers, will find this book helpful in identifying prevailing ethical standards in the profession.

This edition updates the literature and examines a number of emerging issues in more depth (for example, boundary issues, social workers' use of computer technology and involvement in end-of-life decisions). It also includes a new appendix that provides readers with an opportunity to apply the *Code of Ethics* to case scenarios. Chapter 1 provides an overview of ethical issues in social work, relevant historical developments, and the purposes and core contents of the *NASW Code of Ethics*. The remaining chapters focus on the *Code's* standards pertaining to social workers' ethical responsibilities to clients, to colleagues, in practice settings, as professionals, to the social work profession, and to the broader society. The chapters on ethical standards provide a summary and analysis of key ethical issues, often including case examples.

During the years that I have paid serious attention to ethical issues in social work, beginning especially in the mid-1970s, I have been amazed by the exponential growth of interest in the subject among social workers. The reasons for this growth are complex, and they are both reassuring and distressing (see chapter 1). The net result, however, is that contemporary social workers have a better understanding of ethical issues in the profession than did any preceding generation, and that is good. Although I have learned a great deal over the years about these issues, I do not claim to have definitive answers to all ethical quandaries. My hope is that the commentary and analysis in this book will provide readers with thoughtful and thought-provoking guidance as they wrestle with difficult ethical questions and issues. (The views and opinions expressed in this book are my own and do not necessarily reflect the views and opinions of the NASW Code of Ethics Revision Committee or NASW.)

Serving as chair of the NASW Code of Ethics Revision Committee that drafted the code discussed in this book was a genuine privilege. I will always count my work with the esteemed committee members—Carol Brill, Jacqueline Glover, Marjorie Hammock, Vincentia Joseph, Alfred Murillo, Jr., Barbara Varley, and Drayton Vincent—and our principal staff person at NASW, Elizabeth DuMez—among my most treasured professional experiences. This extraordinary group of people spent two years of their professional lives crafting and refining the *Code*. I was awed by and will always appreciate their exceptional dedication, insight, thoughtfulness, and earnestness.

There is no question that the *NASW Code of Ethics* is a vital component of social work's identity and integrity: The *Code* serves as a lodestar for this remarkably diverse profession.

—FREDERIC G. REAMER

Ethical Standards in Social Work
An Introduction

One hallmark of a profession is its willingness to establish ethical standards to guide practitioners' conduct (Callahan & Bok, 1980; Greenwood, 1957; Hall, 1968; Lindeman, 1947). Ethical standards are created to help professionals identify ethical issues in practice and provide guidelines to determine what is ethically acceptable or unacceptable behavior.

Professions typically organize their ethical standards in the form of published codes of ethics (Bayles, 1986; Brandl & Maguire, 2002; Freeman, Engels, & Altekruse, 2004; Kultgen, 1982; Montgomery, 2003). According to Jamal and Bowie (1995), codes of ethics are designed to address three major issues. First, codes address "problems of moral hazard," or instances in which a profession's self-interest may conflict with the public's interest. Such conflicts can occur in a variety of ways. Examples include whether accountants should be obligated to disclose confidential information concerning financial fraud that their clients have committed, whether dentists should be permitted to refuse to treat people who have an infectious disease such as HIV/AIDS, whether physicians should be allowed to invest personally in laboratories or rehabilitation facilities to which they refer patients, and whether social workers should be expected to disclose to law enforcement officials confidential information about crimes their clients have admitted committing.

Second, codes address issues of "professional courtesy," that is, rules that govern how professionals should behave to enhance and maintain a profession's integrity. Examples include whether lawyers should be permitted to advertise and solicit clients, whether psychiatrists should be permitted to engage in sexual relationships with former patients, whether psychologists should be prohibited from soliciting colleagues' clients, and whether social workers should report colleagues who are impaired or who engage in unethical conduct.

Finally, codes address issues that concern professionals' duty to serve the public interest. For example, to what extent should physicians and nurses be expected to assist people when faced with a public emergency? Should dentists donate a portion of their professional time to provide services to low-income people who do not have dental insurance? Should social workers provide services without remuneration to clients whose insurance coverage has been exhausted?

Like other professions—such as medicine, nursing, law, psychology, journalism, and engineering—social work has developed a comprehensive set of ethical standards. These standards have evolved over time, reflecting important changes in the broader culture and in social work's mission, methods, and priorities. They address a wide range of issues, including, for example, social workers' handling of confidential information, sexual contact between social workers and their clients, conflicts of interest, supervision, education and training, and social and political action.

Ethical standards for the social work profession appear in various forms. The *NASW Code of Ethics* (1999; included as an appendix to this book) is the most visible compilation of the profession's ethical standards. Ethical standards also can be found in codes of ethics developed by other social work organizations (for example, the National Association of Black Social Workers [NABSW], the National Federation of Societies for Clinical Social Work [NFSCSW], and the Canadian Association of Social Workers), regulations governing state licensing boards, and codes of conduct promulgated by social services agencies. In addition, the social work literature contains many discussions of ethical norms in the profession (Congress, 1999; Dolgoff, Loewenberg, & Harrington, 2004; Reamer, 1990, 1995a, 1995b, 2006; Rhodes, 1986).

Ethics During Social Work's Early Years

The current *NASW Code of Ethics* reflects major changes in social work's approach to ethical issues throughout its history and the profession's increasingly mature grasp of ethical issues. During the earliest years of social work's history, few formal ethical standards existed. The earliest known attempt to formulate a code was an experimental draft published in the 1920s and attributed to social work pioneer Mary Richmond (Pumphrey, 1959). Although several social work organizations formulated draft codes during the profession's early years—including the American Association for Organizing Family Social Work and several chapters of the American Association of Social Workers—it was not until 1947 that the latter group, the largest organization of social workers of that era, adopted a formal code (Johnson, 1955). In 1960 NASW adopted its first code of ethics, five years after the association was formed. Over time, the *NASW Code of Ethics* has come to be recognized in the United States as the most visible and influential code in social work.

The 1960 *NASW Code of Ethics* consisted of 14 proclamations concerning, for example, every social worker's duty to give precedence to professional responsibility over personal interests; to respect the privacy of clients; to give appropriate professional service in public emergencies; and to contribute knowledge, skills, and support to human welfare programs. First-person statements (that is, "I give precedence to my professional responsibility over my personal interests" and "I respect the privacy of the people I serve") were preceded by a preamble that set forth social workers' responsibility to uphold humanitarian ideals, maintain and improve social work service, and develop the philosophy and skills of the profession. In 1967 a 15th principle pledging nondiscrimination was added to the proclamations.

Soon after the adoption of the code, however, NASW members began to express concern about its level of abstraction, its scope and usefulness for resolving ethical conflicts, and its provisions for handling ethics complaints about practitioners and agencies. As McCann and Cutler (1979) noted,

The sources of dissatisfaction are widespread and have involved practitioners, clients, chapter committees, and, in particular, those persons directly engaged in the adjudication of complaints in which unethical behavior is charged. At a time of growing specialization and organizational differentiation, a variety of issues have surfaced centering on the nature of the code itself, its level of abstraction and ambiguity, its scope and usefulness, and its provision for the handling of ethical complaints. (p. 5)

In 1977 NASW established a task force, chaired by Charles Levy, to revise the code and enhance its relevance to practice; the result was a new code adopted by NASW in 1979. This code included six sections of brief, unannotated principles preceded by a preamble setting forth the code's general purpose and stating that its principles provided standards for the enforcement of ethical practices among social workers:

This code is intended to serve as a guide to the everyday conduct of members of the social work profession and as a basis for adjudication of issues in ethics when the conduct of social workers is alleged to deviate from the standards expressed or implied in this code. It represents standards of ethical behavior for social workers in professional relationships with those served, with colleagues, with employers, with other individuals and professions, and with the community and society as a whole. It also embodies standards of ethical behavior governing individual conduct to the extent that such conduct is associated with an individual's status and identity as a social worker. (NASW, 1979, p. v)

The 1979 code set forth principles related to social workers' conduct and comportment as well as their ethical responsibility to clients, colleagues, employers and employing organizations, the social work profession, and society. The code's principles were both prescriptive (for example, "The social worker should make every effort to foster maximum self-determination on the part of clients" [Principle II.G] and "The social worker should afford clients reasonable access to any official social work records concerning them" [Principle II.H.3]) and proscriptive (for example, "The social worker should not exploit relationships with clients for personal advantage" [Principle II.F 2] and "The social worker should not assume professional responsibility for the clients of another agency or a colleague without appropriate communication with that agency or colleague" [Principle III.K.1]). A number of the code's principles were concrete and specific (for example, "The social worker should under no circumstances engage in sexual activities with clients" [Principle II.F5] and "The social worker should obtain informed consent of clients before taping, recording, or permitting third-party observation of their activities" [Principle II.H.5]), and others were more abstract, asserting ethical ideals (for example, "The social worker should maintain high standards of personal conduct in the capacity or identity as social worker" [Principle I.A] and "The social worker should encourage informed participation by the public in shaping social policies and institutions" [Principle VI.P.7]). Clearly, some principles—especially those pertaining to social justice and general social welfare—were intended to provide social workers with important aspirations, whereas others set forth specific, enforceable standards of conduct, violations of which provided grounds for filing a formal ethics complaint.

The 1979 code was revised twice, eventually including 82 principles. In 1990 several principles related to solicitation of clients and fee splitting were modified after an inquiry into NASW policies by the U.S. Federal Trade Commission (FTC), begun in 1986, that concerned possible restraint of trade. As a result of the inquiry, principles in the code were revised to remove prohibitions concerning solicitation of clients from colleagues or an agency and to modify wording that concerned accepting compensation for making a referral. NASW also entered into a consent agreement with the FTC concerning issues raised by the inquiry.

In 1993 a task force chaired by this author recommended to the NASW Delegate Assembly that it further amend the code of ethics to include five new principles—three related to the problem of social worker impairment and two related to the problem of dual or multiple relationships. This recommendation reflected social workers' growing understanding of the need to address impairment among some social workers and the ways in which blurred or confused boundaries between social workers and clients can compromise the quality of services delivered. The first three of these new principles addressed instances in which social workers' own problems and impairment interfere with their professional functioning, and the latter two addressed the need to avoid social, business, and other nonprofessional relationships with clients because of possible conflicts of interest. The 1993 Delegate Assembly voted to incorporate the five new principles and passed a resolution to establish a task force to draft an entirely new code of ethics that would be far more comprehensive and relevant to contemporary practice, for submission to the 1996 Delegate Assembly.

An entirely new code was needed because, since the 1979 code was drafted, a new scholarly field—applied and professional ethics—had emerged. Much of what contemporary professionals in general and social workers in particular have learned about professional ethics had occurred since the ratification of the 1979 code. Social workers had developed a firmer grasp of the wide range of ethical issues facing practitioners, many of which were not addressed in the 1979 code. The broader field of applied and professional ethics, which had begun in the early 1970s, had matured considerably, resulting in the identification and greater understanding of novel ethical issues not cited in the 1979 code.

For a variety of reasons, especially during the 1980s and early 1990s, scholarly analyses of ethical issues in all professions burgeoned. First, and perhaps most important, was the emergence of complicated ethical issues in health care (for example, public debate about the ethics of allocating scarce organs, genetic engineering, abortion, and euthanasia). These developments led to the establishment of the bioethics field in the late 1960s and early 1970s (Beauchamp & Childress, 2001). Without question, debate and scholarship in bioethics paved the way for other professions' exploration of ethical issues. With bioethics, all professionals began for the first time to appreciate the useful and complex connections between ethical theory and principles and real-life ethical problems faced by practitioners (Reamer, 1985, 1986, 1991a, 1993b, 1997c).

Second, at about the same time (the late 1960s and early 1970s), many social work and health professionals were embroiled in sustained debate concerning patients' rights, welfare rights, prisoners' rights, and civil rights. Relevant issues included a patient's right to refuse treatment, the role of informed consent in research, the humane treatment of prisoners, and affirmative action and civil rights protections in the workplace. These concepts, which many professionals now take for granted, were new at the time, and discussion of them helped shape the emerging field of applied and professional ethics.

Third, professionals began paying more attention to ethical issues because of increased litigation alleging ethical misconduct filed against practitioners in all fields

(Reamer, 2001b). Lawsuits alleging, for example, breaches of privacy and confidentiality, sexual misconduct, defamation of character, fraudulent billing, and inappropriate termination of services alerted many people in the helping professions to possible ethical problems in their ranks. If for no other reason, practitioners needed to learn more about ethics to prevent malpractice claims and avoid lawsuits (Reamer, 2003b).

Fourth, increasingly widespread publicity in all media about professional misconduct did much to convince practitioners that they needed to pay more attention to ethics. For example, there were reports of physicians who committed Medicaid fraud, clergy who were sexually involved with minors, lawyers who raided clients' escrow accounts, police officers who accepted bribes, and psychotherapists who developed sexual relationships with clients. Of course, in the midst of this period (the early 1970s) the nation was wrestling with the ethical implications of the Watergate political scandal, an ethical lapse with far-reaching consequences. Watergate and myriad other national and local political scandals since have done much to inspire interest in ethical issues.

Finally, interest in professional ethics grew because the professions themselves matured. Like people, professions experience stages of development. It took decades for nearly all the professions to pay serious attention to ethical issues, in part because, during the earlier phases of their development, they tended to be preoccupied with cultivating their technical expertise and proficiency. This is understandable, given the professions' need to establish their credibility with the public.

A clear by-product of this general trend is that social workers as a group have begun to pay much more attention to ethical issues in the profession. Many state licensing boards now require ethics education during each licensing cycle. Also, presentations on social work ethics at professional conferences sponsored by NASW, the Council on Social Work Education (CSWE), and other social work organizations have increased substantially. In addition, CSWE has strengthened its requirements concerning instruction in undergraduate and graduate social work education programs on ethical issues and ethical decision making. Moreover, many social services agencies now provide ethics in-service training.

Current *NASW Code of Ethics*

The NASW Code of Ethics Revision Committee was appointed in 1994 and spent two years drafting a new code. This committee, which was chaired by this author and included a professional ethicist and social workers from a variety of practice and educational settings, carried out its work in three phases (Reamer, 1997b). Each phase was designed to provide the committee with the most comprehensive information available on social work ethics and, more broadly, professional ethics, so that the new code would reflect prevailing opinion in the profession.

The committee first reviewed the literature on social work ethics, and applied and professional ethics generally, to identify key concepts and issues that might be addressed in the new code. This was particularly important because so much of the literature on professional and social work ethics had been published after the development of the 1979 code. The committee also reviewed the 1979 code to identify content that should be retained and deleted and to identify areas where content might be added. We then discussed possible ways of organizing the new code to enhance its relevance and use in practice.

During the second phase, and while the first-phase activities were occurring, the committee also issued formal invitations to all NASW members and to members of various social work organizations (such as NABSW, CSWE, NFSCSW, and the Association of Social Work Boards) to suggest issues to be addressed in the new code. The NASW Code of Ethics Revision Committee reviewed its list of relevant content areas drawn from the professional literature and from public comment and developed a number of drafts, the last of which was shared with ethics experts in social work and other professions for their review and comment.

In the third phase, the committee made several revisions based on the feedback we had received from the experts who reviewed the document, published a copy of the draft code in the January 1996 issue of the *NASW News*, and invited all NASW members to send comments to be considered by the committee as it prepared the final draft for submission to the 1996 NASW Delegate Assembly. In addition, during this last phase various committee members met with each of the six NASW Delegate Assembly regional coalitions to discuss the code's development and receive delegates' comments and feedback. The code was then presented to and ratified overwhelmingly by the Delegate Assembly in August 1996 and implemented in January 1997 (NASW, 1996). Since then, NASW has made one modest change to the code.

In 1999 NASW approved deleting a phrase from one standard (1.07[c]) to clarify the circumstances in which social workers may need to disclose confidential information without a client's consent. The deleted phrase required social workers to disclose confidential information "when laws or regulations require disclosure without a client's consent." After the code was ratified in 1996 with this language, some social workers became concerned that this phrase could be interpreted to mean that social workers would be required to comply with new laws requiring disclosure of the identity of undocumented immigrants who were receiving social services, which would compromise practitioners' integrity and erode clients' willingness to trust social workers.

Social Work's Mission

To enhance the code's comprehensiveness, accessibility, and practical relevance, the NASW Code of Ethics Revision Committee departed from the format of the 1979 code. The current code includes four major sections. The first section, "Preamble," summarizes social work's mission and core values. For the first time in NASW's history, the association has adopted and published a formally sanctioned mission statement and an explicit summary of the profession's core values. The committee members believed strongly that it was time for the profession to codify a widely endorsed mission statement, particularly as social work approached the 100th anniversary of its formal inauguration. The mission statement sets forth several themes key to social work practice.

Commitment to Enhancing Human Well-Being and Helping Meet Basic Human Needs of All People. Social work historically has given particular attention to the needs and empowerment of people who are vulnerable, oppressed, and living in poverty. The concept of this enduring dedication to basic human needs was included to remind social workers of the profession's fundamental preoccupation with people's most essential needs, such as food, clothing, health care, and shelter. (See Towle's [1965] seminal work, *Common Human Needs,* for a discussion of this concept.)

Client Empowerment. Especially during the era of charity organization societies in the late 19th and early 20th centuries, many social workers tended to behave paternalistically toward clients. Social workers of that time were inclined to focus on issues of moral rectitude and character in an effort to address people's problems. Over the years, however, as social workers have developed a richer understanding of the ways in which structural problems—such as a weak economy, racial discrimination, poverty, and deindustrialization—can create problems in people's lives, they have promoted client empowerment as a goal (Gutierrez, 1990). *Empowerment* is "the process of helping individuals, families, groups, and communities increase their personal, interpersonal, socioeconomic, and political strength and to develop influence toward improving their circumstances" (Barker, 2003, p. 142). As Black (1994) has suggested,

> Social work has found the concept of empowerment useful for deepening the concerns of the generalist by specifying practice objectives that combine personal control, ability to affect the behavior of others, enhancement of personal and community strengths, increased equity in distribution of resources, ecological assessment, and the generation of power through the empowerment process. The helping relationship is based on collaboration and mutual respect and emphasizes building on existing strengths. (p. 397)

Service to People Who Are Vulnerable and Oppressed. Historically, social workers have been concerned about the well-being of people living in poverty and who are otherwise oppressed. Throughout the profession's history, however, there has been vigorous debate about the extent to which social work must, by definition, focus on the needs of people who are poor and oppressed. In recent years especially, the profession has seen an increase in the number of people interested in obtaining a social work degree to provide clinical mental health services primarily to those who are affluent or covered by third-party insurers (Gibelman, 2005; Popple, 1992; Reamer, 1992a; Siporin, 1992).

The NASW Code of Ethics Revision Committee confronted this issue head on, and the committee's conclusion is reflected in the current code. The mission statement stresses social work's "particular attention to the needs and empowerment of people who are vulnerable, oppressed, and living in poverty." This does not mean that social workers are concerned exclusively with poor and oppressed people. However, it does mean that at social work's core is a fundamental interest in and commitment to people who are poor and oppressed. The committee recognized that many legitimate and important forms of social work address the needs of middle- and upper-income people and those who are eligible for third-party coverage, including social work services provided in schools, hospitals and other health care facilities, mental health agencies, private practice settings, work sites, and the military. However, the committee also asserted that a primary commitment to people who are poor and oppressed is an essential ingredient of social work's mission and identity—an ingredient that distinguishes social work from other helping professions.

Focus on Individual Well-Being in a Social Context. Another defining feature of social work is the profession's earnest attempt to understand and address individuals' problems in a social context. Consistent with the widely embraced ecological perspective (Hartman, 1994), social workers pride themselves in their determination to examine people's problems in the context of their environments, including their families, communities, social networks, employment settings, ethnic and religious affiliations, and so forth. As Compton and Galaway (1994) asserted, the ecological perspective

> offers a conceptual framework that shifts attention from the cause-and-effect relation-ship between paired variables (does the environment cause the person to behave in a cer-tain way, or does the person affect the environment in a certain way?) to the person and situation as an interrelated whole. The person is observed as a part of his or her total life situation; person and situation are a whole in which each part is related to all other parts in a complex way through a complex process in which each element is both cause and effect. These dynamic interactions, transactions, and organizational patterns, which are critical to the functioning of both the individual and the situation, are observable only when we study the whole system. Thus the whole is always more than the sum of its parts. In attempting to understand a problem in social functioning, you cannot achieve under-standing by adding together, as separate entities, the assessment of the individual and the assessment of the environment. Rather you must strive for a full understanding of the complex interactions between client and all levels of social systems as well as the mean-ing the client assigns to these interactions. (p. 118)

Promotion of Social Justice and Social Change. One of social work's hallmarks is its enduring and deep-seated commitment to social justice with and on behalf of clients, "an ideal condition in which all members of a society have the same basic rights, protection, opportunities, obligations, and social benefits" (Barker, 2003, p. 404). Throughout the profession's history, social workers have been actively involved in social efforts to address basic human needs and enhance people's access to important social services. Such social action has taken various forms, such as lobbying public officials, undertaking community organizing, changing organizations to be more responsive, and campaigning for political candidates (Weil & Gamble, 1995). Although social workers' social change efforts have ebbed and flowed over time (Gil, 1994, 1998) at both the national and local levels, at least in principle they have understood the importance of social justice and social action. This, too, is one of the features that distinguishes social work from other helping professions.

Sensitivity to Cultural and Ethnic Diversity. Unlike the earlier NASW codes of ethics, the code emphasizes the need for social workers to understand the role of cultural and ethnic diversity in practice; it also exhorts social workers to strive to end all forms of dis-crimination, whether related to race, ethnicity, gender, or sexual orientation. Particularly since the 1970s, social workers have enhanced their understanding of the ways in which cultural and ethnic norms and history can affect clients' experiences, perceptions, and life circumstances. In addition, social workers have developed a sound understanding of the ways in which social work interventions and social policies must take into consideration cultural and ethnic diversity (Chau, 1991; Devore & Schlesinger, 1998; Green, 1982; Ho, 1987; Hooyman, 1994; Lister, 1987; Lum, 1992; Pinderhughes, 1994).

The preamble to the current code also sets forth the core values in which social work's mission is rooted.

Purpose of the Code

The second section of the code, "Purpose of the NASW Code of Ethics," provides an overview of its main functions and a brief guide for dealing with ethical issues or dilemmas in social work practice. This section alerts social workers to the code's various purposes.

The Code identifies core values on which social work's mission is based. The preamble identifies six core values: service, social justice, dignity and worth of the person, the importance of human relationships, integrity, and competence. The NASW Code of Ethics Revision Committee settled on these core values after a systematic review of literature on the subject. The committee's final list represented a distillation of the numerous lists of social work values proposed by various authors.

The Code summarizes broad ethical principles that reflect the profession's core values and establishes a set of specific ethical standards that should be used to guide social work practice. As discussed in more detail later, the code distinguishes between broad ethical principles based on social work's core values and more specific ethical standards designed to guide practice.

The Code is designed to help social workers identify relevant considerations when professional obligations conflict or ethical uncertainties arise. The code of ethics is one of many tools social workers can use to address ethical issues that emerge in practice. This section's guide for dealing with ethical issues emphasizes various resources social workers should consider when faced with difficult ethical decisions, such as ethical theory and decision making, social work practice theory and research, laws, regulations, agency policies, and other relevant codes of ethics. Social workers are encouraged to obtain ethics consultation when appropriate, whether from an agency-based or social work organization ethics committee, regulatory bodies (for example, a state licensing board), knowledgeable colleagues, supervisors, or legal counsel.

Ethical theory and decision making are now widely understood to be critically important components of practice. Some ethical issues faced by social workers are clear and straightforward. It is easy for practitioners to agree, for example, that clinical social workers should not have sexual contact with clients, social work administrators should not embezzle agency funds, and social work researchers should not fabricate program evaluation results.

Other issues, however, are ethically complex. They arise in situations in which social workers face conflicting professional duties, such that fulfilling one violates another (Reamer, 1990, 1998a, 2006). Examples include social workers who struggle to decide whether to interfere with a client who is engaging in self-destructive behavior; to withhold troubling information contained in a case record from a particularly vulnerable client; to disclose confidential information against a client's wishes to protect a third party from harm; to report to authorities that a professional colleague is impaired or has engaged in unethical behavior; to exaggerate a clinical diagnosis to help a vulnerable client qualify for service; to participate in a labor strike at a work site, which could have detrimental consequences for clients; or to violate a mandatory reporting law to maintain a therapeutic relationship with a client who has made meaningful progress. In such cases, social workers often struggle to reconcile competing and conflicting professional obligations (Reamer, 2005b).

Particularly since the early 1970s, when the field of applied and professional ethics emerged, professionals in all fields have developed a better understanding of the role of ethical theory and ethical decision making in circumstances in which practitioners face conflicting ethical duties (Reamer, 1984, 1987c, 1989b, 1997a, 1998a). During this period social workers began to analyze systematically how practitioners make ethical decisions and resolve ethical dilemmas. Although there have been discussions of ethics and values since the profession's formal beginning in the late 19th century, the deliberate, systematic study of ethical dilemmas in the profession is more recent (Joseph, 1989; Keith-Lucas, 1977; Levy, 1972, 1973, 1976; Reamer, 1995a, 1995b, 2006).

In recent years, practitioners and scholars in many fields have become interested in examining the ways that principles of ethics and ethical theory—drawn largely from the discipline of moral philosophy and, at times, theology—can be applied to ethical dilemmas in the professions. Much of the inquiry has focused on two key questions: (1) What ethical duties do professionals have in relation to clients, colleagues, employers, the social work profession, and the broader society? and (2) What criteria or guidelines can professionals draw on when their ethical duties and responsibilities conflict? (Callahan, 1988; Gambrill & Pruger, 1997; Reamer, 1980, 1982, 1983b, 1993a, 2001a; Reamer & Abramson, 1982; Reid & Popple, 1992).

To approach the analysis of ethical dilemmas deliberately and systematically, social workers and other professionals sometimes draw on theories and principles of ethics. For centuries moral philosophers—sometimes known as "ethicists"—have been developing a wide range of theories and principles concerning issues of right and wrong, the nature of duty and obligation, and justice. Some of these theories focus on issues of metaethics, or debates about whether moral criteria or guidelines can be derived to determine what is ethically right or wrong or good or bad. Some ethicists, known as "cognitivists," believe that "objective" criteria or guidelines can be formulated to assess whether certain actions are or are not ethical; others—"noncognitivists"—assert that ethical judgments will never amount to anything other than subjective opinion or expressions of moral preference (Beauchamp & Childress, 2001; Frankena, 1973; Gewirth, 1978; Reamer, 1989a, 1993a).

Other theories focus on issues of normative ethics, theories intended to guide real-life decisions in ethically complex situations. Not surprisingly, theories of normative ethics have been of particular interest to professionals who face difficult ethical questions. For example, the deontological view claims that certain actions are inherently right or wrong as a matter of principle. Deontologists might argue, for example, that, as a matter of moral obligation, social workers must always obey mandatory reporting laws related to child abuse, even if doing so would jeopardize a social worker's therapeutic relationship with a client—that is, the law is the law (Reamer, 2005b). Similarly, deontologists might argue that clients should always be told the truth, even if knowing the truth might be harmful.

In contrast, the so-called consequentialist, utilitarian, or teleological perspective focuses on the outcome of a course of action and promotes actions that produce the greatest good (Frankena, 1973; Gorovitz, 1971; Smart & Williams, 1973). That is, actions engaged in by professionals are not inherently right or wrong; rather, whether an action is ethical or not is determined by the goodness of its consequences. A proponent of this point of view might argue that, although mandatory reporting laws generally should be followed, because of the good consequences such actions produce, social workers who have evidence to suggest that complying with the law in a particular case would produce harmful consequences (for example, undermining a productive therapeutic relationship) should not comply with the law. The ends can justify the means. Similarly, a proponent of a consequentialist, utilitarian, or teleological perspective might argue that, although clients usually should be told the truth, a social worker who believes that telling a client the truth would cause more harm than good could, on ethical grounds, not tell the client the truth.

Ethicists and professionals continue to disagree about the merits and demerits of these points of view. The debate has been healthy in that it has alerted professionals to competing perspectives that need to be considered when they are faced with an ethical dilemma, especially when professional duties conflict and choices must be made. To enhance the quality of their decision making, social workers need to critically examine the strengths and limitations of various schools of thought that can be brought to bear on the diverse challenges that professional practice produces. This is analogous to the need for clinical social workers to understand the strengths and limitations of the diverse conceptual models used to understand individuals' mental health problems and design interventions to assist them.

The code also highlights the role of ethics consultation. In many cases, practitioners should consult with others when they are faced with challenging ethical dilemmas. Social workers well understand the importance of consultation in other practice domains—for example, when they are unsure where to head clinically in a difficult case, how to handle a complicated administrative matter, or how best to promote a legislative proposal to address a critical issue. Two (or more) heads often are better than one, and this holds for those situations in which ethical dilemmas arise.

Ethics consultation can take various forms. First, social workers should always consider examining the professional literature on ethical issues. Scholarship on social work ethics, and on applied and professional ethics generally, has burgeoned in recent years, and practitioners should do their best to keep up with it. Some of the literature addresses broader, and at times more abstract, issues related to ethical theory and decision-making strategies. Much of it, however, concentrates more narrowly on specific ethical issues, such as the limits of confidentiality when third parties are at risk, informed consent, professional boundaries, and impairment.

Second, many agencies have developed their own ethics committees designed to help staff and clients think through the best way to handle an ethical dilemma. The concept of ethics committees (often called "institutional ethics committees" [IECs]) first emerged in 1976, when the New Jersey Supreme Court ruled that Karen Ann Quinlan's family and physicians should consult an ethics committee in deciding whether to remove her from life support systems. (However, a number of hospitals have had something resembling ethics committees since at least the 1920s.) The New Jersey court based its ruling on an important article by Teel that appeared in the *Baylor Law Review* in 1975 in which a pediatrician advocated the use of ethics committees in cases in which health care professionals face difficult ethical choices.

Ethics committees typically include representatives from various disciplines and positions, such as nursing, medicine, social work, the clergy, and agency administration. Ethics committees in large agencies often include a professional ethicist, typically someone with formal education in moral philosophy and professional ethics. This expert may be a trained philosopher or theologian or a member of one of the professions (for example, a nurse, physician, or social worker) who has supplemental education related to ethics. Sometimes ethics committees also include an agency's attorney. This is especially controversial because an attorney's obligation is to offer advice intended to protect his or her client (in this case, the agency); some critics believe that all members of an ethics committee should be in a position to think freely without constraint. An alternative is to include on the committee an attorney who is not employed by the agency and who, therefore, is free to express more independent opinions based on her or his legal expertise.

Most ethics committees devote the bulk of their time to case consultation (Cohen, 1988; Conrad, 1989; Cranford & Doudera, 1984; Kennedy Institute of Ethics, 1993; Reamer, 1987a). The committee is available to agency staff and perhaps to clients to think through how an ethical dilemma might be handled and to offer nonbinding advice. In health care settings, where ethics committees are particularly prominent, such case consultation might concern the eligibility of a patient for organ transplantation, a patient's right to refuse treatment, and end-of-life decisions. In other settings, such as a community mental health center or family services agency, case consultation might focus on questions concerning the disclosure of confidential information against a client's wishes, whether certain sensitive information should be shared with a particularly fragile client, management of complex boundary and dual relationship issues, and how to handle the discovery of some fraudulent activity within the agency. Although ethics committees are not always able to provide clear-cut advice about the complicated issues that come to their attention (nor should they be expected to), they can provide a valuable forum for thoughtful and critical exploration of complex ethical issues.

Many ethics committees also serve other functions, including drafting, reviewing, and revising agency policies that pertain to ethical issues, such as confidentiality guidelines or informed-consent procedures, and sponsoring staff training on ethics-related matters. Training may include traditional didactic instruction and what has become known in many health care settings as "ethics grand rounds," which are educational sessions offered to staff on various ethics-related topics.

Third, on occasion social workers may want to draw on the expertise of individuals who serve as ethics consultants. These formally educated ethicists can provide useful advice on a case-by-case basis as well as serve as advocates or mediators should the need arise. As with ethics committees, ethics consultants are in a position to help practitioners think through difficult ethical choices, acquaint social workers with relevant conceptual tools and practical resources, and offer nonbinding advice (Aulisio, 2001; Aulisio, Arnold, & Youngner, 2003; Fletcher, 1986; Fletcher, Quist, & Jonsen, 1989; La Puma & Schiedermayer, 1991; Reamer, 1995c; Skeel & Self, 1989; Taylor, 2005).

Of course, consultation can also be obtained from knowledgeable and thoughtful colleagues and supervisors who do not have formal ethics education. In some instances social workers might find it useful to consult with members of their state licensing or regulatory board or members of their NASW chapter's Chapter Ethics Committee (the committee charged with reviewing and adjudicating ethics complaints filed against NASW members). Some NASW chapters also provide more formal ethics consultation services, such as an "ethics hotline."

Finally, social workers should keep in mind that many, although certainly not all, ethical issues broach legal questions that should be brought to the attention of an attorney. For example, social workers may want to seek legal advice when they need to decide whether to disclose confidential information to a third party against a client's wishes, comply with a subpoena that requests privileged information, terminate services to a client who has threatened to file a lawsuit against the social worker, or rely on a deceased client's relative for informed consent purposes in a matter pertaining to the former client.

One key feature of this section of the code is its explicit acknowledgment that circumstances sometimes arise in social work in which the code's values, principles, and standards conflict. The code does not provide a formula for resolving such conflicts and does not specify which values, principles, and standards are most important and ought to outweigh others when they conflict. The code states that

> reasonable differences of opinion can and do exist among social workers with respect to the ways in which values, ethical principles, and ethical standards should be rank ordered when they conflict. Ethical decision making in a given situation must apply the informed judgment of the individual social worker and should also consider how the issues would be judged in a peer review process where the ethical standards of the profession would be applied. . . . Social workers' decisions and actions should be consistent with the spirit as well as the letter of this *Code*. (p. 3)

The Code provides ethical standards to which the general public can hold the social work profession accountable. One defining characteristic of a profession is its members' willingness to provide a mechanism through which the general public can hold the profession accountable (Flexner, 1915; Greenwood, 1957). The *NASW Code of Ethics* sets forth specific ethical standards with which the public can expect social workers to comply and to which the public can hold social workers accountable. Members of the public, particularly clients, who believe that social workers have not complied with the code's standards can file an ethics complaint with NASW. The ethics complaint will be reviewed and, if accepted, adjudicated by a Chapter Ethics Committee or the National Ethics Committee.

The code is particularly relevant in lawsuits involving social workers. Parties that file legal complaints against social workers (for example, former clients or family members) sometimes allege that social workers departed from prevailing ethical standards in social work. A plaintiff in a lawsuit may claim, for example, that a social worker was negligent in failing to obtain informed consent properly before releasing confidential information to a third party, denied a client reasonable access to a case record, failed to protect a third party from harm caused by a client, was sexually involved with a client, or was involved in a harmful business relationship with a client (a conflict of interest). In these instances, lawyers and judges typically draw on the *NASW Code of Ethics* to establish the standard of care in social work. The standard of care—a critically important legal concept in professional malpractice and negligence cases—is defined as how an ordinary, reasonable, and prudent professional would act under the same or similar circumstances (Austin, Moline, & Williams, 1990; Cohen & Mariano, 1982; Madden, 2003; Meyer, Landis, & Hays, 1988; Reamer, 2003b; Schutz, 1982; Stein, 2004). That is, because of the code's prominence and influence nationally—because it has been ratified by the nation's largest social work organization—the code often serves as the measurement rod of what is ethically appropriate and inappropriate in the profession.

There are various ways in which the general public might use the code as a way to hold social workers accountable. In addition to lawyers, courts of law, and professional liability insurance providers, many licensing and regulatory bodies, agency boards of directors, government agencies, and other professional associations adopt the code or portions of it, or they use the code as a frame of reference.

The Code socializes practitioners new to the field to social work's mission, values, ethical principles, and ethical standards. The code provides social work educators, including both classroom faculty and field instructors, with an efficient tool that can be used to acquaint students with the profession's mission, core values, broad ethical principles, and specific ethical standards. It is clearly the most visible and widely recognized statement of social work's aims, values, and ethical principles and standards.

The Code articulates standards that the social work profession itself can use to assess whether social workers have engaged in unethical conduct. The code provides NASW, particularly its ethics committees, with specific standards to determine whether social workers have engaged in unethical conduct. NASW ethics committees are required to use the code as their principal source when complaints are filed against members. As mentioned before, many social work licensing and regulatory boards also use the code or portions of it to adjudicate complaints filed against practitioners who fall under their jurisdiction.

Ethical Principles

The code's third section, "Ethical Principles," presents six broad ethical principles that inform social work practice, one for each of the six core values cited in the preamble. To provide a conceptual base for the profession's ethical standards, the principles are presented at a fairly high level of abstraction. The code also provides brief annotation for each of the principles. It is important to note that the core values on which the ethical principles are based are not listed in rank order: "This constellation of core values reflects what is unique to the social work profession. Core values, and the principles that flow from them, must be balanced within the context and complexity of the human experience" (p. 1).

The first value, service, and the accompanying ethical principle emphasize social workers' commitment to helping people in need. The annotation promotes the concept of altruism, encouraging social workers to "elevate service to others above self-interest" (p. 5). Of special note, social workers are urged but not required to volunteer a portion of their professional skills with no expectation of significant financial return, that is, pro bono service (from the Latin, *pro bono publico,* meaning "for the public good or welfare").

The NASW Code of Ethics Revision Committee concluded that it would be inappropriate to require social workers to volunteer a portion of their professional skills because there are pressing professional and personal demands on many practitioners and their often modest salaries. However, the committee did believe that it was important to encourage social workers to provide some pro bono service.

The second value, social justice, and the accompanying ethical principle reiterate key points made in the code's mission statement. The annotation emphasizes social workers' obligation to pursue social change with, as well as on behalf of, vulnerable and oppressed individuals and groups of people. That is, social workers should not always act for others; when possible, social workers should engage clients and others as partners in efforts to promote social justice and challenge social injustice.

The third value, dignity and worth of the person, and the accompanying ethical principle emphasize the need for social workers to respect people and "treat each person in a caring and respectful fashion, mindful of individual differences and cultural and ethnic diversity" (p. 5). Key elements include promoting clients' "socially responsible self-determination" and enhancing "clients' capacity and opportunity to change and to address their own needs" (pp. 5–6). Thus, although social workers are sensitive to and seek to address structural and environmental determinants of individuals' and social problems, they also understand the important role of individual responsibility. The annotation also acknowledges social workers' dual responsibility to clients and to the broader society and the need for social workers "to resolve conflicts between clients' interests and the broader society's interests in a socially responsible manner" (p. 6).

The fourth value, importance of human relationships, and the accompanying ethical principle stress what social workers have long known, that "relationships between and among people are an important vehicle for change" and that social workers need to "engage people as partners in the helping process" (p. 6). This principle is consistent with and reinforces the discussion of empowerment in the code's mission statement.

The fifth value, integrity, and the accompanying ethical principle emphasize the role of trust in the helping relationship and the need for social workers to "act honestly and responsibly and promote ethical practices on the part of the organizations with which they are affiliated" (p. 6). That is, social workers are not only responsible for their own professional ethics and integrity; they also must seek to ensure that the agencies and organizations with which they are affiliated act ethically and responsibly.

The sixth value, competence, and the accompanying ethical principle assert that social workers should achieve reasonable levels of skill before offering their services to others. This principle exhorts social workers to practice only within their areas of expertise and continually seek to enhance their professional knowledge and skills. The principle also encourages social workers to contribute to the profession's knowledge base.

Ethical Standards

The code's last section, "Ethical Standards," includes 155 specific ethical standards to guide social workers' conduct and provide a basis for adjudication of ethics complaints filed against NASW members. The standards fall into six categories concerning social workers' ethical responsibilities (1) to clients, (2) to colleagues, (3) in practice settings, (4) as professionals, (5) to the profession, and (6) to the broader society. The introduction to this section of the code states that some of the standards are enforceable guidelines for professional conduct and some are standards to which social workers should aspire. This is a very important distinction. Further, "the extent to which each standard is enforceable is a matter of professional judgment to be exercised by those responsible for reviewing alleged violations of ethical standards" (p. 7).

In general, the code's standards concern three kinds of issues (Reamer, 2003b). The first includes what can be described as mistakes social workers might make that have ethical implications. Examples include leaving confidential information displayed on one's desk in such a way that it can be read by unauthorized people or forgetting to include important details in a client's informed-consent document. The second category covers issues associated with difficult ethical decisions, for example, whether to disclose confidential information to protect a third party or whether to continue providing services to an indigent client whose insurance coverage has been exhausted. The final category is concerned with issues pertaining to social worker misconduct, such as exploitation of clients, boundary violations, or fraudulent billing for services rendered.

Ethical Responsibilities to Clients

The first section of the code's ethical standards is the most detailed. It addresses a wide range of issues involved in the delivery of services to individuals, families, couples, and small groups of clients. In particular, this section concerns social workers' commitment to clients, clients' right to self-determination, informed consent, professional competence, cultural competence and social diversity, conflicts of interest, privacy and confidentiality, client access to records, sexual relationships and physical contact with clients, sexual harassment, the use of derogatory language, payment for services, clients who lack decision-making capacity, interruption of services, and termination of services.

Unlike the 1960 and 1979 codes, the current *NASW Code of Ethics* acknowledges that, although social workers' primary responsibility is to clients, circumstances can arise in which "social workers' responsibility to the larger society or specific legal obligations may on limited occasions supersede the loyalty owed clients" (Standard 1.01). For example, this consideration would arise when a social worker is required by law to report that a client has abused a child or has threatened to harm himself or herself or others. Similarly, the code acknowledges that a client's right to self-determination, which social workers ordinarily respect, may be limited when that client's actions or potential actions pose a serious, foreseeable, and imminent risk to himself or herself or others.

Standards for informed consent were added to the current code to specify the elements that should be included when social workers obtain consent from clients or potential clients for the delivery of services; the use of electronic media to provide services (such as computer, telephone, radio, television, and audio- or videotaping clients); third-party observation of clients who are receiving services; and release of information. These standards require the use of clear and understandable language to explain the purpose of services to be provided, risks related to the services, relevant costs, reasonable alternatives, clients' right to refuse or withdraw consent, and the time frame covered by the consent. Social workers also are instructed to inform clients of any limits to services because of the requirements of a third-party payer, such as an insurance or managed care company. This is a critically important provision in light of the growing influence of third-party payers in recent years.

A new section in the code pertains to the subject of cultural competence and social diversity. In recent years social workers have enhanced their understanding of the relevance of cultural and social diversity in their work with clients. Cultural and ethnic norms, for example, may shape clients' understanding of issues in their lives and affect their response to available social services. The code requires social workers to take reasonable steps to understand and be sensitive to clients' cultures and social diversity with respect to race, ethnicity, national origin, color, gender, sexual orientation, age, marital status, political beliefs, religion, or mental or physical disability.

The code's standards concerning conflicts of interest alert social workers to their obligation to avoid circumstances that might interfere with the exercise of professional discretion and impartial judgment. This includes avoiding any dual or multiple relationships with clients or former clients in which there is a risk of exploitation of or other potential harm to the client. Social workers also are urged to take special precautions when they provide services to two or more people who have a relationship with each other. Practitioners who anticipate having to perform in potentially conflicting roles are advised to clarify their obligations with the parties involved and take appropriate action to minimize any conflict of interest (for example, when a social worker is asked to testify in a child custody dispute or divorce proceedings involving clients).

The current code substantially expanded the profession's standards on privacy and confidentiality. Noteworthy details concern social workers' obligation to disclose confidential information to protect third parties from serious harm; confidentiality guidelines for working with families, couples, or groups; disclosure of confidential information to third-party payers; discussion of confidential information in public and semipublic areas (such as hallways, waiting rooms, elevators, and restaurants); disclosure of confidential information during legal proceedings; protection of client confidentiality when responding to requests from the media; protection of the confidentiality of clients' written and electronic records, as well as the confidentiality of information transmitted by use of such devices as computers, electronic mail, fax machines, and telephones; use of case material in teaching or training; and protection of the confidentiality of deceased clients. Social workers are advised to discuss confidentiality policies and guidelines as soon as possible in the social worker–client relationship and then as needed throughout the course of the relationship.

The current code also added considerable detail on social workers' sexual relationships with clients. In addition to prohibiting sexual relationships with current clients, which was addressed in the 1979 code, the current code also generally prohibits sexual contact with former clients. This is a particularly important development because there is intense concern among social workers about practitioners' possible exploitation of former clients. The code also prohibits sexual contact with clients' relatives or other individuals with whom clients maintain a close personal relationship when there is a risk of exploitation of or potential harm to the client. Further, social workers are advised not to provide clinical services to individuals with whom they have had a prior sexual relationship because of the likelihood that such a relationship would make it difficult for the social worker and client to maintain appropriate professional boundaries.

In addition to its greatly expanded detail on sexual relationships, the *NASW Code of Ethics* also comments on other physical contact between social workers and clients. The code acknowledges the possibility of appropriate physical contact (for example, physically comforting a distraught child who has been removed from his home because of parental neglect or holding the hand of a nursing home resident whose spouse has died), but social workers are cautioned not to engage in physical contact with clients, such as cradling or caressing, when there is the possibility that psychological harm to the client could result. Social workers also are admonished not to sexually harass clients.

The current code added a specific provision concerning the use of barter (accepting goods or services from clients as payment for professional service). The code stops short of banning bartering outright, recognizing that in some communities it is a widely accepted form of payment. However, social workers are advised to avoid the use of barter because of the potential for conflict of interest, exploitation, and inappropriate boundaries in their relationships with clients. For example, if a client "pays" a social worker for counseling by performing some service, such as painting the social worker's house or repairing his or her car, and the service is somehow unsatisfactory, attempts to resolve the problem could interfere with the therapeutic relationship and seriously undermine the social worker's effective delivery of counseling services.

In addition to advising social workers to terminate properly with clients when services are no longer required or no longer meet the clients' needs or interests, the code permits social workers in fee-for-service settings to terminate services to clients who have not paid an overdue balance. However, services may be terminated in these circumstances only when the financial arrangements have been made clear to the client, the client does not pose an imminent danger to self or others, and the clinical and other consequences of the client's nonpayment have been discussed with the client.

The code advises social workers who are leaving an employment setting to inform clients of all available options for the continuation of services and their benefits and risks. This is an important standard because it permits a social worker to discuss the advantages and disadvantages associated with a client's decision to continue receiving services from that practitioner in her or his new setting, obtain services from another practitioner in the setting the social worker is leaving, or seek services from a practitioner at some other agency. In addition, the code prohibits social workers from terminating services to pursue a social, financial, or sexual relationship with a client.

Ethical Responsibilities to Colleagues

This section of the code addresses issues concerning social workers' relationships with professional colleagues. These include respect for colleagues; proper handling of shared confidential information; interdisciplinary collaboration and disputes; consultation; referral for services; sexual relationships and sexual harassment; and impaired, incompetent, and unethical colleagues.

The code encourages social workers who are members of an interdisciplinary team, such as in a health care or school setting, to draw explicitly on the perspectives, values, and experiences of the social work profession. If disagreements among team members cannot be resolved, social workers are advised to pursue other ways to address their concerns (for example, approaching agency administrators or board of directors). Social workers are also advised not to exploit disputes between a colleague and an employer to advance their own interests or to exploit clients in a dispute with a colleague.

The current code added a number of standards on consultation and referral for services. Social workers are obligated to seek colleagues' advice and counsel whenever such consultation is in the client's best interest, disclosing the least amount of information necessary to achieve the purposes of the consultation. Social workers also are expected to keep informed of colleagues' areas of expertise and competence. In addition, they are expected to refer clients to other professionals when colleagues' specialized knowledge or expertise is needed to serve clients fully, or when they believe they are not being effective or making reasonable progress with clients.

This section of the code also addresses dual and multiple relationships, specifically with respect to prohibiting sexual activities or contact between social work supervisors or educators and those supervised, whether they are students, trainees, or other colleagues over whom they exercise professional authority. In addition, the code prohibits sexual harassment of supervisees, students, trainees, or colleagues.

The current code strengthens ethical standards pertaining to impaired, incompetent, and unethical colleagues. Social workers who have direct knowledge of a colleague's impairment (which may be the result of personal problems, psychosocial distress, substance abuse, or mental health difficulties, and which interferes with practice effectiveness), incompetence, or unethical conduct are required to consult with that colleague when feasible and assist him or her in taking remedial action. If these measures do not address the problem satisfactorily, social workers are required to take action through appropriate channels established by employers, agencies, NASW, licensing and regulatory bodies, and other professional organizations. Practitioners also are expected to defend and assist colleagues who are unjustly charged with unethical conduct.

Ethical Responsibilities in Practice Settings

This section of the code addresses ethical issues that arise in social services agencies, human services organizations, private practice, and social work education programs. The standards pertain to social work supervision and consultation, education and training, performance evaluation, client records, billing for services, client transfer, agency administration, continuing education and staff development, commitments to employers, and labor–management disputes.

One major theme in this section of the code is that social workers who provide supervision, consultation, education, or training should do so only within their areas of knowledge and competence. Also, social workers who provide these services are to avoid engaging in any dual or multiple relationships in which there is a risk of exploitation or potential harm. Another standard requires social workers who are educators or field instructors to ensure that clients are routinely informed when services are being provided by students.

Several standards pertain to client records. They require that records include sufficient, accurate, and timely documentation to facilitate the delivery of services and ensure continuity of services provided to clients in the future. Documentation in records should protect clients' privacy to the greatest extent possible and appropriate and should include only information that is directly relevant to the delivery of services. In addition, the code requires social workers to store records properly to ensure reasonable future access and notes that records should be maintained for the number of years required by state statutes or relevant contracts.

Social workers who bill for services are obligated to establish and maintain practices that accurately reflect the nature and extent of services provided, and they must not falsify billing records or submit fraudulent invoices.

Social workers are urged to be particularly careful when an individual who is receiving services from another agency or colleague contacts them for services. They should carefully consider the client's needs before agreeing to provide services. To minimize possible confusion and conflict, social workers should discuss with such a potential client the nature of his or her current relationship with other services providers and the implications, including possible benefits or risks, of entering into a relationship with a new provider. If a new client has been served by another agency or colleague, social workers should discuss with the client whether consultation with the previous provider is in the client's best interest.

The current code greatly expands coverage of ethical standards for agency administration. The code obligates social work administrators to advocate within and outside their agencies for adequate resources to meet clients' needs and provide appropriate staff supervision; they also must promote resource allocation procedures that are open and fair. In addition, administrators must ensure that the working environment for which they are responsible is consistent with and encourages compliance with the *NASW Code of Ethics,* and they should provide or arrange for continuing education and staff development for all staff for whom they are responsible.

The code also includes a number of ethical standards for social work employees. Although these employees are generally expected to adhere to commitments made to their employers and employing organizations, they should not allow an employing organization's policies, procedures, regulations, or administrative orders to interfere with their ethical practice of social work. Thus, a social worker is obligated to take reasonable steps to ensure that his or her employing organization's practices are consistent with the *NASW Code of Ethics*. Also, social workers should accept employment or arrange students' field placements only in organizations with fair personnel practices. Practitioners should conserve agency funds where appropriate and must never misappropriate funds or use them for unintended purposes.

A novel feature of the code is its acknowledgment of ethical issues that social workers sometimes face as the result of labor–management disputes. Although the code does not prescribe how social workers should handle such dilemmas, it does permit them to engage in organized action, including the formation of and participation in labor unions to improve services to clients and working conditions. The code states that "reasonable differences of opinion exist among social workers concerning their primary obligation as professionals during an actual or threatened labor strike or job action" (Standard 3.10[b]).

Ethical Responsibilities as Professionals

This section of the code focuses on issues related to social workers' professional integrity. The standards pertain to social workers' competence, obligation to avoid any behavior that discriminates against others, private conduct, honesty, personal impairment, and solicitation of clients.

In addition to emphasizing social workers' obligation to be proficient, the code exhorts practitioners routinely to review and critique the professional literature; participate in continuing education; and base their work on recognized knowledge, including empirical knowledge, relevant to social work practice and ethics.

Several standards address social workers' values and personal behavior. The code states that social workers should not practice, condone, facilitate, or collaborate with any form of discrimination and should not permit their private conduct to interfere with their ability to fulfill their professional responsibilities. Thus, for example, it would be unethical for a social worker who has racist views to campaign for political office, publicize her or his social work credentials, and publicly espouse explicitly racist social policies—this would violate the code's standard on discrimination. In addition, this private conduct would likely interfere with the social worker's ability to fulfill his or her professional responsibilities, assuming that the racist views become well known among clients and colleagues and reflect on the social worker's professional life.

The code further obligates social workers to make clear distinctions between statements and actions engaged in as a private individual and as a social worker. For example, a social work administrator who volunteers to be a spokesperson for a candidate for political office should make it clear that he or she is involved in the political activities in his or her personal, not professional, capacity (unless the social worker's employer or board of directors has authorized him or her to endorse and support the candidate on the agency's behalf).

A prominent theme in the code concerns social workers' obligation to be honest in their relationships with all parties, including accurately representing their professional qualifications, credentials, education, competence, and affiliations. Social workers should not exaggerate or falsify their qualifications and credentials, and they should claim only those relevant professional credentials that they actually possess (for example, a social worker who has a doctorate in physics should not claim to have or create the impression that he or she has a doctoral degree relevant to clinical social work). Also, social workers are obligated to take responsibility and credit, including authorship credit, only for work they have actually performed and to which they have contributed. For example, they should not claim to have had a prominent role in a research project to which they contributed minimally. In addition, social workers should honestly acknowledge the work of and the contributions made by others. It would be unethical for a social worker to draw on or benefit from a colleague's work without acknowledging him or her.

The code also requires that social workers not engage in uninvited solicitation of potential clients who, because of their circumstances, are vulnerable to undue influence, manipulation, or coercion. Thus, social workers are not permitted to approach vulnerable people in distress (for example, victims of a natural disaster or serious accident) and actively solicit them to become clients. Further, social workers must not solicit testimonial endorsements (that is, for advertising or marketing purposes) from current clients or from other people who, because of their particular circumstances, are vulnerable to undue influence.

One of the most important standards in the code concerns social workers' personal impairment. Like all people, social workers sometimes encounter personal problems—this is a normal part of life. The code mandates, however, that social workers must not allow their personal problems, psychosocial distress, legal problems, substance abuse, or mental health difficulties to interfere with their professional judgment and performance or to jeopardize others for whom they have a professional responsibility. When social workers find that their personal difficulties interfere with their professional judgment and performance, they are obligated to seek professional help, make adjustments in their workload, terminate their practice, or take other steps necessary to protect clients and others.

Ethical Responsibilities to the Social Work Profession

Social workers' ethical responsibilities are not limited to clients, colleagues, and the public; they also include the social work profession itself. Standards in this section of the code focus on the profession's integrity and social work evaluation and research. The principal theme concerning the profession's integrity pertains to social workers' obligation to maintain and promote high standards of practice by engaging in appropriate study and research, teaching, publication, presentations at professional conferences, consultation, service to the community and professional organizations, and legislative testimony.

In recent years social workers have strengthened their appreciation of the role of evaluation and research. Relevant activities include needs assessments, program evaluations, clinical research and evaluations, and the use of empirical literature to guide practice. The current code added a substantially new series of standards concerning evaluation and research. These standards emphasize social workers' obligation to monitor and evaluate policies, the implementation of programs, and practice interventions. In addition, the code requires social workers to critically examine and keep current with emerging knowledge relevant to social work and use evaluation and research evidence in their professional practice.

The code also requires social workers involved in evaluation and research to follow widely accepted guidelines concerning the protection of evaluation and research participants. The standards concentrate on the role of informed consent procedures in evaluation and research, the need to ensure that evaluation and research participants have access to appropriate supportive services, the confidentiality and anonymity of information obtained during the course of evaluation and research, the obligation to report results accurately, and the handling of potential or real conflicts of interest and dual relationships involving evaluation and research participants.

Ethical Responsibilities to the Broader Society

The social work profession has always been committed to social justice. This commitment is clearly reflected in the "Preamble" to the *NASW Code of Ethics* and in the final section of the code's standards. The standards explicitly emphasize social workers' obligation to engage in activities that promote social justice and the general welfare of society "from local to global levels" (Standard 6.01). These activities may include facilitating public discussion of social policy issues; providing professional services in public emergencies; engaging in social and political action—such as lobbying and legislative activity—to address basic human needs; promoting conditions that encourage respect for the diversity of cultures and social diversity; and acting to prevent and eliminate domination, exploitation, and discrimination against any person, group, or class of people.

Conclusion

Ethical standards in social work—particularly as reflected in the *NASW Code of Ethics*—have changed dramatically during the profession's history. During the late 19th and early 20th centuries, social work's ethical standards were sparse and generally vague.

Along with all other professions, and largely as a result of the emergence of the applied and professional ethics field that began in the 1970s, social work's ethical standards have matured considerably. The current *NASW Code of Ethics* reflects social workers' increased understanding of ethical issues in the profession and the need for comprehensive ethical standards.

However, ethical standards in social work cannot guarantee ethical behavior. Such standards can guide practitioners who encounter ethical challenges and establish norms by which social workers' actions can be judged. In the final analysis, however, ethical standards in general, and a code of ethics in particular, are only one part of social workers' ethical arsenal. In addition to specific ethical standards, social workers need to draw on ethical theory and decision-making guidelines; social work theory and practice principles; and relevant laws, regulations, and agency policies. Most of all, social workers need to consider ethical standards within the context of their own personal values and ethics. As the *NASW Code of Ethics* states, ethical principles and standards "must be applied by individuals of good character who discern moral questions and, in good faith, seek to make reliable ethical judgments" (p. 4).

2

Ethical Responsibilities to Clients

T he standards in this section of the code concern social workers' relationships with individual clients, couples, families, and small groups. They focus on the nature of social workers' commitment to clients, client self-determination, informed consent, social workers' competence to work with clients, cultural competence and social diversity, conflicts of interest, privacy and confidentiality, client access to records, sexual relationships between social workers and (current and former) clients and clients' relatives or other individuals with whom they maintain a close personal relationship, physical contact with clients, sexual harassment of clients, social workers' use of derogatory language, client payment for services, serving clients who lack decision-making capacity, interruption of services, and termination of services.

Commitment to Clients

STANDARD 1.01

Social workers' primary responsibility is to promote the well-being of clients. In general, clients' interests are primary. However, social workers' responsibility to the larger society or specific legal obligations may on limited occasions supersede the loyalty owed clients, and clients should be so advised. (Examples include when a social worker is required by law to report that a client has abused a child or has threatened to harm self or others.)

Social workers have long recognized that their primary responsibility is to their clients, and their clients' interests are primary. Most often, social workers' responsibility to their clients is clear and straightforward. As this standard suggests, however, instances can arise when social workers find themselves caught between their clients' and the broader society's interests. Here are several common examples:

- A social worker, a caseworker in a family services agency, was told by her client (who was in counseling because she was having difficulty managing her child's behavior) that the client had lost control the day before and injured her child's arm while "dragging her to her room." The client had made impressive progress in treatment after having been referred to the social worker by the county child welfare department, whose staff had received reports of possible child abuse in the home. The client pleaded with the social worker not to report the most recent incident to the child welfare authorities.

- A 17-year-old boy, a client in a residential program for adolescents with emotional and behavioral difficulties, told his social worker during a counseling session, "I'm tired of life's hassles and want to end it all. I know you might think I'm just asking for help, but I'm not. I've had it, and I want to say good-bye. Please don't do anything to stop me." After extensive exploration, the social worker concluded that the client was serious about wanting to commit suicide.

- A social worker in a community mental health center provided counseling to a 32-year-old man who was separated from his wife. According to the client, his wife had had an affair with another man. In a fit of rage, the client told the social worker that he was planning to "really do a number on my wife and her lover. They'll rue the day they decided to ruin my life like this." The client blurted out to the social worker that he had hired someone to physically harm both his wife and her lover. When the social worker pressed the client for details, the client joked and said, "You don't know whether I'm serious or not, do you?" Given the client's well-known penchant for domestic violence, the social worker believed that he could very well carry out the threat.

These examples illustrate how social workers might find themselves torn between their commitment to their clients and their obligation to protect clients from themselves (when there is a threat of injury to self or suicide) or to protect third parties from harm (when clients threaten others). The 1979 *NASW Code of Ethics* stated, "The social worker should make every effort to foster maximum self-determination on the part of clients" (Principle II.G, p. 5). The code did not acknowledge possible conflicts between clients' interests and social workers' responsibility to the larger society or obligation to comply with specific legal requirements. In contrast, the current code recognizes that such conflicts can occur and that clients have the right to be informed about this possibility. This is a fact of professional life, and social workers must accept that circumstances may arise in which they will have to make choices—sometimes difficult ones—that compromise clients' immediate interests.

Social workers have developed considerable understanding of how such conflicts can occur and the ways to deal with them. For example, since the 1960s, social workers throughout the United States have been required to disclose confidential information, sometimes against a client's wishes, to comply with mandatory reporting laws on child and elder abuse and neglect. Although many social workers were initially concerned about the possible impact of these reporting requirements, particularly with respect to the possibility that they would erode clients' trust in social workers, in general the profession has come to accept that professional responsibility entails reconciling occasional conflicts between their clients' and others' interests. Certainly such mandatory reporting requirements have the potential to alter clinical relationships between social workers and clients; nonetheless, social workers now recognize the public's compelling interest in this social policy and the need for social workers to balance their commitment to clients with their commitment to the larger society.

Generally, situations involving possible conflict between the interests of clients and others fall into three groups. First, there are circumstances in which clients' interests clearly should prevail—for example, when a client informs his social worker that seven years earlier he committed a relatively minor crime. Although there might be some benefit to the public if the social worker were to disclose this information to law enforcement officials (so the client could be prosecuted), current ethical norms and public policy clearly suggest that, overall, such a disclosure would produce more harm than good, particularly with respect to the public's willingness to trust social workers. Social workers generally agree that in such cases they should not place the public's interests above clients' interests.

Second, there are circumstances in which clients' interests clearly are outweighed by the public's interests or by some legal requirement. An obvious example would involve a client who asks his social worker not to notify child welfare authorities that he has been sexually involved with his 11-year-old stepdaughter. In this case, the social worker has an obligation to protect the vulnerable child. Third, sometimes it may not be clear whether the client's or the public's interests, or a legal requirement, should take precedence—for example, when a client informs a social worker that he or she recently committed a moderately serious offense or has been inconsistent in caring for an elderly and incapacitated parent (i.e., when it is not clear whether the client has been neglectful). In these situations, reasonable social workers may disagree about the nature of their ethical duties to the various parties involved.

These are among the most difficult ethical choices facing social workers. They illustrate why social workers need to be familiar with relevant ethics literature, the role of ethics consultation, and ethical decision-making strategies. Practitioners who encounter such ethical dilemmas would be well advised to check the literature for information about the arguments for and against various courses of action (for example, disclosing confidential information concerning clients' past criminal activity and complying with mandatory reporting laws); consult with colleagues who are knowledgeable about the ethical issues involved (for example, social workers, members of allied professions and, when necessary and appropriate, lawyers); and acquaint themselves with ethical decision-making models to help them organize their thinking, thoroughly consider the key ethical issues (and relevant philosophical or conceptual perspectives), and reach a conclusion (Congress, 1999; Dolgoff et al., 2004; Reamer, 1995a, 2006).

As an example of this process, consider a social worker whose HIV-positive client has been unwilling to share this information with his sexual partner. The social worker used various clinical approaches in an attempt to bring the client to a point at which he was willing to inform his partner about his medical condition. Unfortunately, the clinical strategy failed, and the social worker had to decide whether to disclose confidential information against the client's wishes and alert the client's partner to the potential risk (including the possibility that the partner was already infected).

The practitioner faced a complicated ethical dilemma. The social worker had to decide whether to respect the client's wish for confidentiality and privacy or disclose confidential information to protect a third party—a classic example of conflicting ethical duties. The social worker had exhausted all the clinical options to help the client reach a point at which he was willing to share the information with his partner (which are often, but not always, effective ways to address such an issue), so the social worker needed to become acquainted with the relevant literature on confidentiality of information pertaining to HIV infection and the disclosure of confidential information to protect third parties (see, for example, Bennett & Erin, 2001; Francis & Chin, 1987; Gray & Harding, 1988; Kain, 1988; Reamer, 1991a, 1991b). The social worker also needed to consult with knowledgeable colleagues and supervisors and an ethics committee, if one was available. An attorney's advice would be especially useful with respect to relevant statutes and case law, particularly concerning the tension between confidentiality rights and professionals' obligation to protect third parties (and associated liability risks for the social worker).

In addition, it would be particularly helpful for a social worker in this situation to be familiar with various ethical theories that might help him or her sort out important conceptual points (for example, comparing and contrasting deontological and utilitarian arguments in this case could be especially useful). Of course, the social worker also should examine all of the relevant standards in the *NASW Code of Ethics* (for example, pertaining to client self-determination and confidentiality limits) and carefully document his or her various decision-making efforts in the case record. In the final analysis, a social worker facing this kind of difficult decision—where professionals in the field disagree about the most appropriate course of action or standard of care—needs to make the ethical decision as carefully and deliberately as possible, taking into consideration as much information as possible. This is the approach that is most likely to protect the social worker's client, third parties, and the social worker himself or herself.

Self-Determination

STANDARD 1.02

Social workers respect and promote the right of clients to self-determination and assist clients in their efforts to identify and clarify their goals. Social workers may limit clients' right to self-determination when, in the social workers' professional judgment, clients' actions or potential actions pose a serious, foreseeable, and imminent risk to themselves or others.

This standard is related to the preceding standard concerned with social workers' commitment to clients. Standard 1.02 makes it clear that, in general, social workers should respect clients' right to self-determination. However, this standard acknowledges explicitly that there are potential limits to clients' right to self-determination, particularly when clients "pose a serious, foreseeable, and imminent risk to themselves or others." As with the standard on social workers' commitment to clients, this standard moves beyond the language of the 1979 code that concerned clients' right to self-determination.

This standard on client self-determination reflects social workers' increased understanding of two key concepts: (1) professional paternalism and (2) protection of third parties. *Professional paternalism* means that situations may arise in which social workers have an obligation to protect clients from themselves. In his classic statement on the subject, Dworkin (1971) defined *paternalism* as "interference with a person's liberty of action justified by reasons referring exclusively to the welfare, good, happiness, needs, interests, or values of the person being coerced" (p. 108).

The most extreme form of self-injurious behavior is, of course, client suicide, and social workers generally agree that professionals have a duty to interfere with clients' efforts to end their lives (although there is some debate among social workers about the ethics of euthanasia and physician-assisted suicide; see Foster, 1995). But there are other, more subtle forms of self-harming behavior that pose difficult ethical dilemmas for social workers. How assertive should social workers be with battered women or men who decide to resume a relationship with an abusive partner? Should social workers interfere with hospital patients who want to return home while they are still in very frail condition and acting against medical advice? To what extent should social workers provide clients with access to information about themselves that is likely to be harmful to the clients?

In these "gray areas," reasonable practitioners may disagree, and it is important for social workers to understand the concept of professional paternalism. The debate concerning the obligation to protect people from themselves is an ancient one, dating back at least to Aristotle's time (Reamer, 1983a). Contemporary debate about the nature and limits of paternalism is especially intense because of widespread concern with civil rights and liberties. Controversy about paternalistic treatment of people with mental illness, children, welfare recipients, senior citizens, and prisoners has stimulated much philosophical and judicial speculation about the limits of coercion. This debate demonstrates the tension between social workers who believe in clients' right to identify and pursue their own goals, take risks, and possibly make mistakes and those who believe that at least some degree of coercion or deception is justifiable if it is necessary to protect clients from harming themselves.

Paternalism is such a difficult problem for social workers because most practitioners are drawn to the profession by a sincere wish to help people who are experiencing difficult problems in their lives—for example, people with clinical depression, who are suicidal, who are living in unsanitary housing, who are involved in abusive relationships, or who are addicted to drugs or alcohol. That is, limits on professional paternalism may run counter to many practitioners' instincts to protect vulnerable people from engaging in self-destructive behavior.

Issues involving the protection of third parties are quite different. Here the justification for social workers' placing limits on clients' right to self-determination is based on social workers' explicit concern for other people whose well-being is threatened by a client's actions. Unlike cases involving professional paternalism, when social workers are primarily concerned about the client's well-being, circumstances calling for limits on clients' right to self-determination to protect third parties are those in which social workers must concede that protection and promotion of clients' interests is a secondary consideration.

The concept of interfering with clients' right to self-determination to protect third parties is usually associated with the often-cited case of *Tarasoff v. Board of Regents of the University of California* (1976). This case set the precedent for a number of critically important statutes and court decisions that now influence social workers' decisions when clients pose a threat to third parties.

In 1969 Prosenjit Poddar, an outpatient at Cowell Memorial Hospital at the University of California at Berkeley, informed his psychologist, Dr. Lawrence Moore, that he was planning to kill an unnamed young woman (easily identified as Tatiana

Tarasoff) on her return to the university from her summer vacation. After the counseling session during which Poddar announced his plan, Moore notified the university police and asked them to observe Poddar because he might need hospitalization as an individual who was dangerous to himself or others. The psychologist followed the telephone call with a letter requesting the help of the chief of the university police.

The campus police temporarily took Poddar into custody but released him because there was evidence that he was rational. They also warned him to stay away from Tarasoff. Poddar then moved in with Tarasoff's brother in an apartment near Tarasoff's home, where she lived with her parents. Shortly thereafter, Moore's supervisor and the chief of the department of psychiatry, Dr. Harvey Powelson, asked the university police to return the psychologist's letter about Poddar, ordered that the letter and the psychologist's case notes be destroyed, and directed that no further action be taken to hospitalize Poddar. No one warned Tarasoff or her family of Poddar's threat. Poddar never returned to counseling. Two months later, he murdered Tarasoff.

Tarasoff's parents sued the university board of regents, several employees of the student health service, and the chief of the campus police, along with four of his officers, because their daughter was never notified of Poddar's threat. A lower court in California dismissed the suit on the basis of sovereign immunity of the multiple defendants and the psychotherapist's need to preserve confidentiality. The parents appealed, and the California Supreme Court upheld the appeal and later reaffirmed the appellate court's decision that failure to protect the intended victim was irresponsible. The California Supreme Court ultimately held that

> when a therapist determines, or pursuant to the standards of his profession should determine, that his patient presents a serious danger of violence to another, he incurs an obligation to use reasonable care to protect the intended victim against such danger. The discharge of this duty may require the therapist to take one or more of various steps, depending upon the nature of the case. Thus it may call for him to warn the intended victim or others likely to apprise the victim of the danger, to notify the police, or to take whatever other steps are reasonably necessary under the circumstances. . . . We recognize the public interest in supporting effective treatment of mental illness and in protecting the rights of patients to privacy, and the consequent public importance of safeguarding the confidential character of psychotherapeutic communication. Against this interest, however, we must weigh the public interest in safety from violent assault. . . . We conclude that the public policy favoring protection of the confidential character of patient–psychotherapist communications must yield to the extent to which disclosure is essential to avert danger to others. The protective privilege ends where the public peril begins. (551 P .2d 334 at 336–337)

Without question, *Tarasoff* changed the way mental health practitioners think about the limits of clients' right to self-determination and confidentiality rights. Since *Tarasoff*, a number of important duty-to-protect cases have influenced courts and legislatures in situations concerning mental health professionals' duty to protect third parties. Many court decisions reinforce the court's conclusions in *Tarasoff*, emphasizing practitioners' responsibility to take reasonable steps to protect third parties when, in the professionals' judgment, clients' actions or potential actions pose a serious, foreseeable, and imminent risk to others. Other cases, however, challenge, extend, or otherwise modify the conclusions reached in *Tarasoff*. I examine these issues more fully in the discussion of confidentiality.

Informed Consent

STANDARD 1.03(a)

Social workers should provide services to clients only in the context of a professional relationship based, when appropriate, on valid informed consent. Social workers should use clear and understandable language to inform clients of the purpose of the services, risks related to the services, limits to services because of the requirements of a third-party payer, relevant costs, reasonable alternatives, clients' right to refuse or withdraw consent, and the time frame covered by the consent. Social workers should provide clients with an opportunity to ask questions.

Social workers have always recognized the importance of informed consent, whether it pertains to the release of information, provision of services, medication, or audio or video recording (Bernstein, 1960; Keith-Lucas, 1963; McDermott, 1975; Perlman, 1965; Reamer, 1987b). The current standard concerning informed consent reflects what professionals have learned in recent years about the nature of the consent process, particularly in light of various important court decisions involving parties who questioned the validity of consent obtained by professionals.

The first major legal ruling in the United States on informed consent is found in the 1914 landmark decision of *Schloendorff v. Society of New York Hospital*, in which New York Supreme Court Justice Benjamin Cardozo set forth his opinion concerning an individual's right to self-determination: "Every human being of adult years and sound mind has a right to determine what shall be done with his own body" (cited in Pernick, 1982, pp. 28–29). To do otherwise, Cardozo argued, is to commit an assault upon the person.

Another important decision was handed down in the 1957 case of *Salgo v. Leland Stanford Jr. University Board of Trustees*, in which the term *informed consent* was formally introduced. The plaintiff in this case, who became paraplegic following a diagnostic procedure for a circulatory problem, claimed that his physician did not properly disclose ahead of time pertinent information concerning risks associated with the procedure.

Although the concept of informed consent has its origins in medicine and health care, over the years it has been applied legislatively, judicially, and administratively to a wide range of other client groups, such as people with mental illness or disability, children, senior citizens, people with physical disabilities, prisoners, hospital patients, and research participants (Schutz, 1982).

States and local jurisdictions have different interpretations of informed-consent standards, but there is considerable agreement about a number of key elements, and these are reflected in Standard 1.03(a):

- Coercion and undue influence must not have played a role in the client's decision.
- Clients must be mentally capable of providing consent and able to understand the language and terms used during the consent process.
- Clients must consent to specific procedures or actions, not to broadly worded or blanket consent forms.
- The forms of consent must be valid (although some states require written authorization, most recognize both written and oral consent).

- Clients must have the right to refuse or withdraw consent.
- Clients' decisions must be based on adequate information: details of the nature and purpose of a service or disclosure of information; advantages and disadvantages of an intervention; substantial or probable risks to clients, if any; potential effects on clients' families, jobs, social activities, and other important aspects of their lives; alternatives to the proposed intervention or disclosure; and anticipated costs for clients and their relatives. All this information must be presented to clients in understandable language and in a manner that encourages them to ask questions. Consent forms also should be dated and include an expiration date. Social workers should be especially sensitive to clients' cultural and ethnic differences related to the meaning of such concepts as "self-determination" and "consent" (Berg, Applebaum, Lidz, & Parker, 2001; Cowles, 1976; Dickson, 1995; Faden & Beauchamp, 1986; President's Commission, 1982; Reamer, 1987b, 2003b; Rozovsky, 1984).

There are various circumstances in which social workers may not be required to obtain informed consent (Dickson, 1995; Rozovsky, 1984). The most important involve emergencies. In genuine emergencies, professionals may be authorized to act without the client's consent. According to many state statutes and case law, an emergency entails a client's being incapacitated and unable to exercise the mental ability to make an informed decision. Interference with decision-making ability might be the result of injury or illness, alcohol or drug use, or any other disability. In addition, a need for immediate treatment to preserve life or health must exist. Many statutes also authorize practitioners to treat clients without their consent to protect the client or the community from harm. Cases involving substance abusers, prisoners, and people with sexually transmitted diseases are examples (Appelbaum, Lidz, & Meisel, 1987; Dickson, 1995; President's Commission, 1982; Rozovsky, 1984).

A special feature of Standard 1.03(a) is its reference to social workers' obligation to inform clients of any "limits to services because of the requirements of a third-party payer." This clause empowers social workers who are pressured by third-party payers (insurers) to withhold information from clients about the third-party payers' internal policies concerning covered services, reimbursement for services rendered, and so on. Consistent with social work's long-standing commitment to clients' right to know, this part of the standard enables social workers to resist any efforts on the part of third-party payers to withhold information from clients that concerns limits to services (sometimes referred to as "gag orders").

STANDARD 1.03(b)

In instances when clients are not literate or have difficulty understanding the primary language used in the practice setting, social workers should take steps to ensure clients' comprehension. This may include providing clients with a detailed verbal explanation or arranging for a qualified interpreter or translator whenever possible.

Clearly, clients who are not literate or have difficulty understanding the primary language used in the practice setting would not be able to provide informed consent unless social workers take steps to ensure comprehension. In one case, a hospital-based social worker and a doctor spoke with the parents of a two-year-old child who had died during an emergency medical procedure. The parents were from a Southeast Asian culture who emigrated to the United States and had difficulty understanding English. Despite the parents' limited English, the social worker and doctor had the parents sign an informed-consent form authorizing the hospital to perform an autopsy on the child. When the parents realized that an autopsy had been performed, they were distraught because the procedure violated their strongly held religious beliefs. The couple ultimately filed a lawsuit alleging that the social worker and doctor had failed in their responsibility to take reasonable steps to ensure that they understood the nature of the informed-consent form that they were asked to sign.

Reasonable steps is a broad term open to varying interpretation. Ordinarily, such steps include providing a detailed oral explanation to someone who is not literate or arranging for a qualified interpreter or translator when clients have difficulty understanding the primary language used in the practice setting. Social workers should be aware that some clients who are able to speak the primary language used in the practice setting reasonably well (expressive language skill) may not be equally capable of understanding the language (receptive language skill).

Social workers also should be aware of cultural and ethnic differences with respect to the concept of informed consent. For example, Hahn stated that "the individualism central in the doctrine of informed consent is absent in the tradition of Vietnamese thought. Self is not cultivated, but subjugated to cosmic orders. Information, direct communication, and decision may be regarded as arrogant" (cited in President's Commission, 1982, pp. 55–56). In contrast, Harwood (cited in President's Commission, 1982) noted that Puerto Rican Hispanics in the mainland United States expect to be engaged in the therapeutic process and want information provided to them without condescension. Social workers should take such cultural and ethnic differences into account when they obtain clients' informed consent; some clients may feel less comfortable with the process than others and thus require more patience and reassurance.

STANDARD 1.03(c)

In instances when clients lack the capacity to provide informed consent, social workers should protect clients' interests by seeking permission from an appropriate third party, informing clients consistent with the clients' level of understanding. In such instances social workers should seek to ensure that the third party acts in a manner consistent with clients' wishes and interests. Social workers should take reasonable steps to enhance such clients' ability to give informed consent.

This standard focuses primarily on clients with diminished capacity to give informed consent, as a result of, for example, mental disability, mental illness, substance abuse, or brain injury. In such cases, social workers should attempt to obtain informed consent from an individual who is authorized to act on the client's behalf. This may be a relative, guardian, or some other individual who has legal authority to provide consent.

Social workers must remember that, although clients may lack the capacity to provide informed consent (because of a permanent disability or temporary incapacity), clients retain the right to receive information about the purposes of consent consistent with their level of understanding and comprehension. Consider, for example, a 32-year-old patient in a rehabilitation facility following a serious accident at the construction site where he worked. As a result of the accident, the patient sustained permanent brain damage that severely limited, but did not completely eliminate, his ability to process and retain new information.

During the patient's stay at the rehabilitation center, a social worker received a request from his former employer for information related to the patient's mental impairment (in connection with the former employer's processing of the patient's disability claim). The social worker was required to obtain informed consent before forwarding this clinical information. Because of the patient's disability, she spoke with the patient's wife about providing consent. However, the social worker also sat down with the patient and, in the simplest language possible, explained to him that his former employer had requested information about how he was doing. That is, although the social worker obtained consent from "an appropriate third party," she also informed her client of the request for confidential information in a way that was consistent with the client's level of understanding.

Sometimes it is easy to determine whether a client is sufficiently competent to provide informed consent. Clearly, clients in the midst of a floridly psychotic episode, when there is strong evidence of delusions and hallucinations, would not be considered competent to provide informed consent. Other cases are less clear, however. In general, social workers should not presume that certain client groups—such as children, elderly people, and those with a mental illness or disability—are necessarily incompetent (except those who are unconscious). Rather, clients in some categories, such as adults with severe mental disabilities or children manifesting psychotic symptoms, should be considered to have a greater probability of incapacity (Reamer, 2003b). As Rozovsky (1984) stated, it is important that professionals not assume "that a person who has consumed a moderate amount of alcohol or drugs or who has a history of psychiatric problems is automatically incapable of giving consent: the facts and circumstances of individual cases are essential to such determinations" (p. 89). Rozovsky also noted that clinicians should keep in mind that clients' capacity to provide informed consent may fluctuate over time; individuals who are incompetent at one point may be capable of giving (or withdrawing) consent during a subsequent lucid phase.

Assessments of a client's capacity should include such measures as a mental status examination (evaluation of a person's orientation to person, place, time, situation, mood and affect, content of thought and perception), the ability to comprehend abstract ideas and make reasoned judgments, any history of mental illness that might affect current judgment, and the client's recent and remote memory. When clients are deemed incompetent, social workers should be guided by what is known as the principle of *substituted judgment* or *proxy judgment*, according to which an appropriate third party, or surrogate, attempts to replicate the decision that the incompetent client would make if able to make a sound decision (President's Commission, 1982). (For an extensive discussion of these concepts, see Buchanan & Brock, 1990.) According to Standard 1.03(c), social workers must seek to ensure that "the third party acts in a manner consistent with clients' wishes and interests." Thus, social workers should be alert to possible conflict of interest when a third party relied on for substituted or proxy judgment places his or her own self-interest above the client's interests.

A social worker who believes that the relative or acquaintance of an incompetent client, who has the authority to consent on the client's behalf, is acting in a manner that is undermining the client's interests, would be obligated to take steps to ensure that this issue is addressed (perhaps by bringing this concern to the attention of the client's attorney). For example, a social worker employed in a nursing home provided casework services to an 82-year-old man who was not able to provide his own informed consent. The client developed several life-threatening health problems, and the medical staff needed to decide how aggressively they should treat his condition. The client's wife, who had the authority to provide consent on his behalf, told the social worker and medical staff that she did not want her husband treated aggressively. The social worker, however, had doubts about the wife's motives. The social worker knew from her conversations with the client that the marriage had been strained for years. In the social worker's judgment, the client's wife might have been eager for her husband to die so that she would be eligible to receive his sizable insurance benefits. The nursing home administrator and the social worker consulted with the nursing home's lawyer about how to handle the possible conflict of interest.

Finally, social workers who need to obtain informed consent from a third party for an incapacitated client also are obligated to enhance the client's ability to provide informed consent. Sometimes, little can be done to improve clients' capacity to provide informed consent—for example, when clients have a profound mental disability or have permanent and extensive brain damage. In other cases, however, social workers may be in a position to enhance clients' ability to give informed consent—for example, when clients are hospitalized as a result of an acute episode of clinical depression or drug overdose. With appropriate services, these clients might very well regain their ability to provide informed consent without the formal involvement of a third party acting on their behalf.

STANDARD 1.03(d)

In instances when clients are receiving services involuntarily, social workers should provide information about the nature and extent of services and about the extent of clients' right to refuse service.

There are a number of circumstances in which social workers' clients receive services involuntarily. Most notable are clients who are hospitalized involuntarily in a psychiatric facility or who are incarcerated.

There has been extensive debate among professionals, as well as litigation, about involuntary clients' right to refuse service. For example, with respect to life-saving treatment, the recent general trend is that a competent adult has the right to refuse services and treatment, particularly when the client has no dependents and his or her friends or family agree with the decision to refuse treatment; the treatment is highly intrusive or exceptionally painful; the treatment is risky, experimental, or has a small chance of success; the quality of the patient's life will be seriously affected by the treatment or by the medical condition even with the treatment; the treatment will only postpone imminent death; or the client has deeply held religious beliefs opposing the treatment. However, treatment may be mandated against the client's wishes if the client has minor children or other dependents; the treatment would be a relatively minor intrusion or involve a relatively minor invasion of bodily integrity; the proposed treatment is a generally accepted type of treatment; the quality of the client's life would not be adversely affected by the treatment or if the client would not live a limited or painful life following treatment; or the treatment would not merely prolong the client's life for a short time but would actually save the client's life (Saltzman & Proch, 1990; Stein, 2004).

Courts also may deny a client the right to refuse treatment when the client is a danger to himself or herself or others. In *Rennie v. Klein* (1978), for example, a U.S. District Court ruled that involuntary psychiatric patients may have the right to refuse medication or other forms of treatment in the absence of an emergency, consistent with the constitutional right to privacy. To overrule the patient's refusal, four factors should be considered by an objective independent party: (1) the patient's capacity to decide on his or her particular treatment, (2) the patient's physical threat to other patients and staff, (3) whether any less-restrictive treatment exists, and (4) the risk of permanent side effects from the proposed treatment.

When clients receive treatment or services involuntarily for whatever reason, social workers should provide them with as much information as possible about the nature of the treatment or services they will receive and the extent of their right to refuse treatment or service. Consistent with the obligation to respect clients' right to socially responsible self-determination (Standard 1.02), social workers should assist clients who wish to assert their right to refuse treatment or services, keeping in mind the simultaneous obligation to protect both clients and third parties from harm. Social workers may need to seek legal advice about any given client's legal right to refuse treatment or services.

STANDARD 1.03(e)

Social workers who provide services via electronic media (such as computer, telephone, radio, and television) should inform recipients of the limitations and risks associated with such services.

Social workers are now in a position to use various forms of electronic media in their work with clients. Some of these media, such as telephone, radio, and television, have been used in social work for many years. For example, in addition to the many familiar uses of the telephone, some social workers also use radio and television for professional purposes. They are hosts of or guests on radio call-in shows, during which listeners call for on-the-air advice about personal or family problems. Similarly, social workers are hosts of or guests on television programs that address mental health issues; these broadcasts also sometimes provide an opportunity for viewers to telephone in for on-the-air advice concerning issues in their lives. Some social workers also use video conferencing to provide services to clients who live far from where the social workers practice.

Social workers also have taken advantage of advances in computer technology to provide professional services, including information, counseling, and referral services via the Internet. Because of continuing rapid developments in the computer industry, it is likely that social workers' use of computer technology to provide professional services will increase.

Clearly, computer-based technology has many potential benefits. In addition to enhancing clients' access to information, many social workers can provide valuable services via the Internet. For example, clinical social workers can use the Internet to reach clients who are unable to come into their office because of geographical distance or emotional barriers (such as an anxiety disorder). But, computer technology also brings with it significant risks.

Practitioners who provide professional services by use of electronic media must be aware of and routinely inform recipients (who may or may not be formal clients) about the limitations and risks associated with such services. First, recipients should know that the information and advice they receive via electronic media may be superficial. For example, a social worker who hosted a radio call-in show received a call from a man who reported experiencing major anxiety symptoms (heart palpitations, excessive sweating, dizziness, shortness of breath). The social worker talked with the caller on the air about the nature of anxiety disorders and panic attacks. She also described several common therapeutic techniques used to reduce anxiety (for example, systematic desensitization, cognitive therapy). At no time during the conversation, however, did the social worker alert the caller to possible alternative diagnoses (known formally as differential diagnosis), such as substance-induced anxiety disorder or other anxiety and psychotic disorders that have panic attacks as an associated feature. She also did not encourage the caller to seek a local qualified professional for a thorough assessment. As a result, the social worker exposed herself to ethical and legal risk.

A second risk is that social workers who provide clinical services via the Internet do not have access to important visual cues that provide meaningful information during face-to-face encounters with clients. Social workers who communicate with clients via e-mail, for example, cannot see pained expressions on clients' faces, tears trickling down their cheeks, or angry looks. This could affect a social worker's ability to form an effective therapeutic alliance with clients.

A third risk, particularly in relation to the use of computer-linked services, is breach of privacy. Recipients of services provided by social workers on the Internet, for example, should be informed that, given the current state of computer technology, it is possible that computer-based communications will be seen by others who know how to intercept messages or "eavesdrop" electronically. In one case, a social worker who communicated with a client via e-mail did not realize that he had accidentally selected an option in his software that resulted in sending his message to the client, which contained identifying information, to a list of people in his computer-based address book. Consequently, many people who should not have been privy to the communication had access to it, exposing the social worker to the possibility of an ethics complaint or lawsuit.

Finally, social workers who have only electronic contact with clients may not know for certain that their clients are who they say they are. This would be particularly problematic in a crisis situation. The social worker would have difficulty directing help to the client.

Social workers can take several practical steps to protect clients:

1. Develop a clear, comprehensive statement that fully discloses the possible benefits and risks of the services they provide via electronic media.
2. Provide clients with detailed and complete assessment tools, along with a statement of how important it is for the client to be forthright in completing these tools.

3. Be aware of all security precautions needed to prevent hacking, misdirecting e-mails, eavesdropping on telephone conversations, and more.
4. Obtain from the client the name of a contact person and also outline a clear emergency plan.
5. Check for applicable statutory regulations with the state board of social work examiners and, if the client lives in another state, with the board in the client's state.
6. If communicating by text-based message on the Internet, provide communication tips to facilitate clearer understanding with the client.

STANDARD 1.03(f)

Social workers should obtain clients' informed consent before audiotaping or videotaping clients or permitting observation of services to clients by a third party.

Social workers audiotape or videotape clients, or services provided to them, in various circumstances. First, they may audiotape or videotape clients for purposes of supervision. That is, their supervisors, colleagues, or members of a peer supervision group may listen to or view tapes of work with clients to provide informed feedback. Second, social workers may audiotape or videotape clients for teaching purposes—for example, to use in a class at a school of social work or at a professional conference or workshop. Third, clients may be taped for research purposes. Social workers who conduct in-depth research interviews, for example, may prefer to audiotape the dialogue for later transcription to avoid taking copious notes during the interview and distracting the respondent. Fourth, social workers may audiotape or videotape for clinical purposes. For example, sometimes social workers may want clients to view videotapes of themselves to obtain feedback on their communication style, behavior, or nonverbal mannerisms. Finally, social workers may audiotape or videotape clients for marketing purposes, that is, to include in an advertisement, public service announcement, or broadcast used to publicize a particular agency, program, or service.

In addition to audiotaping and videotaping, on occasion social workers may want to permit third parties to observe clients, either in person or through a one-way mirror. Practitioners who administer a residential mental health program, for example, may want to invite local public officials, media representatives, or financial contributors to tour the facility and see it "in action."

In all these cases, social workers must be aware of potential violations of clients' privacy. Some clients may feel strongly about their privacy, and social workers have an obligation to protect it as much as possible. Thus, social workers should always obtain clients' informed consent before taping or permitting observation of services to clients by a third party. Consistent with Standard 1.03(a), social workers should use clear and understandable language to inform clients of the purpose of the taping or observation, any associated risks (for example, who exactly will view the tapes or participate in the observation), reasonable alternatives (if any), clients' right to refuse or withdraw consent, and the time frame covered by the consent. Social workers also should provide clients with an opportunity to ask relevant questions. In addition, special provisions should be made for clients who are not literate or who have difficulty understanding the primary language used in the practice setting (Standard 1.03[b]) or who lack the capacity to provide informed consent (Standard 1.03[c]).

Competence

STANDARD 1.04(a)

Social workers should provide services and represent themselves as competent only within the boundaries of their education, training, license, certification, consultation received, supervised experience, or other relevant professional experience.

Social work is a remarkably diverse profession. It includes clinicians and caseworkers, community organizers, supervisors, administrators, advocates and community activists, policy makers, educators, program evaluators, and researchers. What practitioners have in common is formal social work education and at least one social work degree (undergraduate, graduate, or both).

Social workers must be forthright and clear in their claims about their areas of competence and expertise to colleagues, potential employers, and the public at large. They must not misrepresent their competence for self-serving purposes—for example, to obtain employment or attract clients. There are many examples. A social worker who has been out of graduate school for just a year and has not yet been licensed as an independent clinical social worker should not promote himself or herself as a clinician with years of post-master's-degree experience. Practitioners who have considerable education and expertise related to substance abuse treatment should not claim expertise they do not have in other clinical areas, such as treatment of eating disorders, just as social workers who have not received formal training in suicide prevention techniques should not provide this service to clients. Similarly, a social worker who has never conducted an ambitious program evaluation and has not received extensive training in that area should not claim such expertise in a grant proposal submitted to a foundation to obtain funds.

STANDARD 1.04(b)

Social workers should provide services in substantive areas or use intervention techniques or approaches that are new to them only after engaging in appropriate study, training, consultation, and supervision from people who are competent in those interventions or techniques.

New and interesting innovations that may be relevant to practitioners' work are constantly emerging. Social workers should be aware of and seek education and training about new developments in the field that may be appropriate to incorporate into work with clients. For example, clinical social workers should continually update their knowledge of intervention techniques related to their areas of expertise. Administrators should be aware of new management models and strategies. Program evaluators should be familiar with new approaches to documenting the outcome and effectiveness of services.

According to Standard 1.04(b), social workers who provide substantive services or use intervention techniques should do so only after appropriate study, training, consultation, and supervision. Sometimes independent education may suffice—for example, when a social worker who has considerable experience working with cancer survivors reviews the literature about new clinical social work approaches in oncology treatment, or when an experienced program evaluator learns from a journal article about a new tool to measure client progress.

In other cases, however, social workers may need to obtain formal training, continuing education, consultation, or supervision to begin work in a new substantive area or use a new intervention technique. For example, a clinical social worker who wants to concentrate on "recovered memories" in work with traumatized clients should obtain proper training, consultation, and supervision before doing so. This may involve attending workshops and conferences on the subject and joining a peer consultation or supervision group to learn about the proper use of this approach and to address any clinical risks.

Social workers who obtain training, consultation, or supervision need to ensure that the trainers, consultants, and supervisors themselves are competent. There should be reasonable assurance that they have the requisite substantive expertise the social workers are seeking (specific knowledge about the subject) and the ability to provide effective education, training, consultation, and supervision. Sometimes, colleagues who are very well informed about a subject are not particularly skilled at teaching others or providing useful consultation or supervision. Social workers should be selective, just as clients should be when they seek out social work services.

For example, a social worker in private practice was interested in the use of hypnosis in work with clients diagnosed with eating disorders. The social worker read several books and journal articles about hypnosis and then began using the technique with selected clients, but he did not attend any workshops, institutes, or continuing education seminars. One of the social worker's clients filed an ethics complaint and lawsuit against the social worker, alleging that the social worker had emotionally abused and traumatized the client during hypnosis sessions. The social worker was vulnerable because he could not demonstrate that he had engaged in proper study before using hypnosis with clients.

STANDARD 1.04(c)

When generally recognized standards do not exist with respect to an emerging area of practice, social workers should exercise careful judgment and take responsible steps (including appropriate education, research, training, consultation, and supervision) to ensure the competence of their work and to protect clients from harm.

Social workers who want to use intervention approaches or techniques that are new to them are the primary focus of Standard 1.04(b). In other cases, however, social workers may want to use an intervention approach or technique that is new to the profession. For example, some professional conferences have featured presentations on the use of so-called "reparenting therapy" as a treatment for adult survivors of childhood sexual abuse. According to the philosophy behind this treatment approach, clients who were traumatized as children were often neglected by their parents, deprived of appropriate and much-needed nurturing and caretaking. Thus, an important goal of therapy with such clients would be to provide them an opportunity in adulthood to experience being cared for by competent "parents"—that is, a therapist who functions as a surrogate parent. As part of the therapeutic relationship, the counselor may prepare meals or purchase food and clothing for the client, arrange for the client's medical care when the need arises, or take the client out for recreation and entertainment (such as going to a movie or a ballgame). Such activities are intended to help the client experience what it is like to be cared for by a loving parent.

There are no generally recognized standards for this treatment approach. Such an approach would generate controversy among social workers because potential boundary issues might arise (see Standard 1.06[c]). Although some social workers may endorse use of reparenting therapy techniques, many others would be reluctant to use them.

Because it remains controversial, social workers who contemplate using this approach would be wise to exercise extraordinarily careful judgment and take responsible steps to protect clients from harm. Before using any techniques that are new to the field, practitioners should spend considerable time reading the relevant literature, consulting with colleagues, attending workshops or continuing education seminars, and obtaining appropriate supervision. In particular, social workers should attempt to locate empirical literature documenting the effectiveness of such an approach (see Standards 4.01[c] and 5.02[c]). One possible result is that social workers will conclude that using a controversial new treatment approach is too risky, ethically and clinically.

Some emerging areas of practice do not raise particularly complicated ethical issues. For example, a social worker interested in the use of a new cognitive therapy technique to address self-esteem issues may not face complex ethical issues. In this kind of situation it may suffice for the social worker to read the relevant literature, consult with colleagues, attend workshops or seminars, and obtain appropriate supervision. In other cases, as in the use of reparenting therapy, social workers need to add another step: exploring in considerable depth the ethical issues connected to the intervention approach. In the case of reparenting therapy, the social worker would need to take a hard look at potential problems pertaining to boundary issues that could emerge and harm the client.

Cultural Competence and Social Diversity

STANDARD 1.05(a)

Social workers should understand culture and its function in human behavior and society, recognizing the strengths that exist in all cultures.

Especially since the 1970s, social workers' understanding of the relevance of cultural competence and social diversity has matured. They have developed an appreciation of the various ways in which clients' cultures, including their ethnic and cultural backgrounds and sexual orientation, affect practice. First, culture and ethnicity may influence how individuals cope with life's problems and interact with each other (Chau, 1991; Devore & Schlesinger, 1998; Green, 1982; Ho, 1987; Hooyman, 1994; Lister, 1987; Lum,

1992; Pinderhughes, 1994). Phenomena such as mental illness, the use of mood-altering substances, and death have different connotations in different cultural and ethnic groups. What is behaviorally appropriate in one culture (for example, talking to deceased relatives) may seem abnormal in another. Accepted practice in one culture (such as shaking hands upon meeting a member of the opposite sex) may be prohibited in another. Active participation in an informed-consent procedure in a social services agency may be expected in one culture and considered odd in another. Clearly, to fully understand and appreciate these differences, social workers must be familiar with varying cultural traditions and norms.

Second, clients' cultural backgrounds may affect their interest in seeking professional services in the first place (Devore & Schlesinger, 1998; Lum, 1992). Some cultural groups may have a preference for informal problem solving that takes place within the local ethnic community. For historical or other reasons, some cultural groups may not trust professionals who offer services in the context of formal agencies. Understanding the dynamics of this preference may be helpful to social work administrators and program directors who want to enhance their delivery of services to specific cultural groups.

In addition, the ways in which social services are planned and implemented may affect their effectiveness within particular cultural groups (Boyd-Franklin, 1989; Devore & Schlesinger, 1998). Self-disclosure in the context of a treatment group, placement of a family member in a nursing home, or use of psychotropic medication may be unacceptable or even abhorrent to members of some cultural groups. Social workers must take this variation into account as they plan and deliver services.

It is especially important for social workers to understand how some widely accepted theories of human behavior have fostered destructive stereotypes or have been based on limited samples of people that do not include important cultural and ethnic groups or minorities. Psychodynamic theories (Sigmund Freud), ego psychology theories (Anna Freud, Heinz Hartmann, Robert White, Margaret Mahler, Erik Erikson), learning theory (B. F. Skinner, Albert Bandura), cognitive theory (Jean Piaget), interpersonal theory (Alfred Adler, Harry Stack Sullivan), and humanistic theory (Abraham Maslow) have been critiqued because of their lack of attention to issues of cultural and ethnic diversity (Beckett & Johnson, 1995).

An important element of this ethical standard concerns social workers' obligation to recognize the strengths that exist in all cultures. Practitioners need a solid understanding of various cultural groups' positive and functional coping patterns, traditions, and customs. Social workers must understand that cultural practices that are different from those of the majority culture are not, by definition, counterproductive or dysfunctional. Rather, differences among cultural groups should be celebrated and accounted for in social work practice (Freeman, 1990; Leashore, 1995; Weick, Rapp, Sullivan, & Kristhardt, 1989). As Schlesinger and Devore (1995, p. 903) stated,

> As various groups send their children to school, become ill, encounter marital difficulties, and generally live their lives, they bring with them a unique ethnic and class tradition. . . . As they confront "helpers" or "caretakers" they expect . . . that these aspects of their being . . . will be understood [whether or not they are aware that] some of their strengths and tensions are related to this aspect of their lives.
>
> Those charged with the responsibility of . . . helping have the obligation to be sensitive to that possibility.

STANDARD 1.05(b)

Social workers should have a knowledge base of their clients' cultures and be able to demonstrate competence in the provision of services that are sensitive to clients' cultures and to differences among people and cultural groups.

In recent years, a number of social work professionals have outlined content related to cultural and social diversity that is essential knowledge for their colleagues. Pinderhughes (1994), for example, recommended that social workers be informed about clients' culture as a factor in problem formation, problem resolution, and the helping process itself, which includes assessment, relationship development, intervention, and evaluation of outcome:

> The specific perspectives, capacities, competencies, and abilities that facilitate such effectiveness, and which are mandatory for cultural competence, include:
>
> 1. knowledge of the specific values, beliefs, and cultural practices of clients;
> 2. the ability to respect and appreciate the values, beliefs, and practices of all clients, including those culturally different, and to perceive such individuals through their own cultural lenses instead of the practitioner's;
> 3. the ability to be comfortable with difference in others and thus not be trapped in anxiety about difference or defensive behavior to ward it off;
> 4. the ability to control, and even change, false beliefs, assumptions, and stereotypes, which means one will have less need for defensive behavior to protect oneself;
> 5. the ability to think flexibly and to recognize that one's own way of thinking and behaving is not the only way; and
> 6. the ability to behave flexibly. This is demonstrated by the readiness to engage in the extra steps required to sort through general knowledge about a cultural group and to see the specific ways in which knowledge applies or does not apply to a given client. These steps take extra time, effort, and energy. (p. 266)

Schlesinger and Devore (1995) have offered a compelling outline of essential knowledge pertaining particularly to ethnicity, which includes knowledge about relevant values (both social workers' and clients'); theories of human behavior that concern cultural and ethnic groups; relevant social welfare policies and services; self-awareness (thinking through and feeling the impact of one's ethnicity on one's perception of self and others); and the impact of the "ethnic reality" on individuals' willingness to seek and receive social services, and the ways in which services are designed and delivered.

This kind of knowledge can be helpful to social workers in various settings and circumstances. For example, social workers in health care settings and programs for elders (hospitals, home health care agencies, nursing homes, senior day care programs) need to be familiar with differences among cultural and ethnic groups with respect to blood transfusions, autopsies, and what is assumed to happen to a person following death (such as concepts of the afterlife) and how these differences may affect clients' preferences and choices. Social workers in family services agencies and community mental health centers may need to be familiar with various cultural groups' religious beliefs and observance of religious holidays, particularly as they affect scheduling of programs and services. Practitioners in programs that serve abused and battered women need to be aware of varying cultural norms concerning the role of women in society and in marriage and other intimate relationships. Social workers in treatment programs for children and adolescents may need to be knowledgeable about the perception and treatment of gay men, lesbians, and bisexual men and women by members of different cultural and ethnic groups.

It is not sufficient, of course, for social workers to be knowledgeable about clients' cultures. They also need to be able to demonstrate competence in the provision of services that are sensitive to clients' cultures and to differences among people and cultural groups. In addition to professional experience, such competence can be achieved through formal social work education (both classroom and field education), in-service training in social services agencies, professional workshops and conferences, consultation, and supervision. As Schlesinger and Devore (1995) asserted, culturally sensitive practice

> is manifested at the level of daily practice behavior. It represents the capacity to draw on assumptions and facts about diverse ethnic groups in problem solving. Social workers should demonstrate the capacity to move with each client at a pace and in a direction determined by the client's perception of the problem. (p. 906)

STANDARD 1.05(c)

Social workers should obtain education about and seek to understand the nature of social diversity and oppression with respect to race, ethnicity, national origin, color, sex, sexual orientation, age, marital status, political belief, religion, and mental or physical disability.

Social workers' efforts to understand and be knowledgeable about culture and ethnicity should focus especially on the concept of social diversity in all its forms and the role of oppression in the lives of members of culturally diverse groups. This need has been recognized by the Council on Social Work Education (CSWE), particularly with respect to populations at risk. In its *Educational Policy and Accreditation Standards* (2004), CSWE asserted that

> social work programs integrate content that promotes understanding, affirmation, and respect for people from diverse backgrounds. The content emphasizes the interlocking and complex nature of culture and personal identity. It ensures that social services meet the needs of groups served and are culturally relevant. Programs educate students to recognize diversity within and between groups that may influence assessment, planning, intervention, and research. Students learn how to define, design, and implement strategies for effective practice with persons from diverse backgrounds. (p. 9)

The concept of *oppression* is particularly important in social work, especially because of its relevance to the experience of members of ethnic groups, people of color, and members of other socially nondominant groups. According to Gil (1994),

> Oppression refers to relations of domination and exploitation—economic, social, and psychologic—between individuals; between social groups and classes within and beyond societies; and, globally, between entire societies. . . . Oppression seems motivated by an intent to exploit (i.e., benefit disproportionately from the resources, capacities, and productivity of others), and it results typically in disadvantageous, unjust conditions of living for its victims. It serves as means to enforce exploitation toward the *goal* of securing advantageous conditions of living for its perpetrators. (p. 233)

As Standard 1.05(c) suggests, ideally, social workers obtain education themselves about various forms of diversity, including those related to race, ethnicity, national origin, color, gender, sexual orientation, age, marital status, political belief, religion, and mental or physical disability. This is an impressive amount of knowledge to grasp. Realistically, it may not be possible for social workers to master all this information at the beginning of their careers. What is important is that they recognize the need to obtain this knowledge throughout their careers and take steps to gain it when it is essential for their work.

Conflicts of Interest

STANDARD 1.06(a)

Social workers should be alert to and avoid conflicts of interest that interfere with the exercise of professional discretion and impartial judgment. Social workers should inform clients when a real or potential conflict of interest arises and take reasonable steps to resolve the issue in a manner that makes the clients' interests primary and protects clients' interests to the greatest extent possible. In some cases, protecting clients' interests may require termination of the professional relationship with proper referral of the client.

Ethical issues involving actual or potential conflicts of interest are among the most complex faced by social workers. Conflicts of interest occur when a social worker's services to or relationship with a client is compromised, or might be compromised, because of decisions or actions in relation to another client, a colleague, himself or herself, or some other third party (Madden, 2003; Stein, 2004). According to Gifis (1991), a *conflict of interest* involves "a situation in which regard for one duty leads to disregard of another . . . or might reasonably be expected to do so" (p. 88). Conflicts of interest may be actual or potential (when conflicting interests may develop but do not yet exist).

Conflicts of interest can occur in every profession—for example, a lawyer represents two clients charged with the same crime and exposing the guilt of one party may exonerate the other; a physician stands to benefit financially by ordering diagnostic tests for a patient and referring the patient to a laboratory in which the physician has a personal investment; a journalist covers a public scandal in which a close relative is allegedly involved; and a public official is responsible for regulating a utility in which she owns a substantial amount of stock.

Conflicts of interest in social work can take several forms. They may occur in the context of social workers' relationships with clients or in their roles as community organizers, supervisors, consultants, administrators, policy officials, educators, researchers, or program evaluators. Social workers must be careful to avoid conflicts of interest that might harm clients because of their decisions or actions involving other clients, colleagues, themselves, or other third parties. For example, a social worker employed by the state department of corrections administered the prison system's sexual offender treatment program. He conducted treatment groups for inmates convicted of crimes such as child molestation, rape, and other forms of sexual assault. When inmates were eligible for parole, the social worker made recommendations to the parole board concerning each inmate's readiness for parole and, for those deemed ready, services that should be mandated as a condition of parole. These recommendations usually included specific provisions for follow-up counseling.

In addition to his duties as an employee of the state department of corrections, the social worker also was a partner in a community-based group psychotherapy practice. In several cases. he recommended to the state parole board that inmates be referred to this group practice after their release from prison, but he did not disclose his own affiliation with the practice. This case involved a conflict of interest because the social worker had an incentive to refer inmates to his group practice, from which he might benefit personally.

In another case, a social worker in private practice was married to a man who owned a small manufacturing firm. On occasion the social worker's husband would become aware of his employees' personal problems that were interfering with their work, such as problems related to their marriages or alcohol use. The social worker's husband gave these employees his wife's business card and encouraged them to consult with her about their problems, and he did not provide information about other providers or agencies. These situations involved a conflict of interest in several important ways. First, there was a potential clash between a client's best interests, in a clinical sense, and the employer's (the social worker's husband's) financial interests. That is, the clinical goals could lead to a course of action that would cause a valuable employee to resign from his or her job or ask for a leave of absence, contrary to the needs of the social worker's husband. Second, the social worker might have a financial stake in how she handles the client's employment-related issues. That is, a client's decisions and actions with respect to his or her job with the social worker's husband could have an impact on the family's finances, and this could affect the social worker's judgment. Third, the employees' receipt of social work services provided by their employer's wife may undermine their trust that confidentiality would be respected.

In such circumstances when potential conflicts of interest arise, social workers have an obligation to be alert to and avoid actual or potential conflicts of interest that might interfere with the exercise of their professional discretion and impartial judgment. Practitioners should resolve the conflict in a manner that makes the clients' (or potential clients') interests primary and protects clients' interests to the greatest extent possible. For example, the prison-based social worker who referred sex offenders to the group psychotherapy practice should have disclosed to corrections officials that he was involved in that practice. He should not have referred inmates to the practice because of the possibility that he would benefit from such referrals. It is possible that the social worker would have referred parole-eligible inmates to that practice in part because of the possibility of his own financial gain rather than the inmates' clinical needs. Instead, the social worker should have referred clients to practitioners with whom he was not affiliated, and there would have been no risk of a conflict of interest. If this social worker and his colleagues were the only appropriate local providers of follow-up services for sex offenders, the social worker should have negotiated an explicit agreement with department of corrections officials to avoid any conflict of interest. For example, he could have implemented a comprehensive services delivery plan that included an institutional component and a community-based component, a plan structured in such a way that there would be no financial incentive for the social worker to refer inmates to the practice with which he was affiliated.

The social worker who received referrals from her husband should have explained to him the inappropriateness of such referrals and helped him refer employees to other services providers (perhaps by contracting with an employee assistance program [EAP] that would screen and refer to providers in the community).

Issues of conflict of interest can be extremely complex, so it is helpful to examine several other examples involving actual or potential conflicts:

- A social worker in community organizing was working with a group of elderly residents in a low-income neighborhood to address affordable housing problems among elderly people in the area. The social worker, who was very knowledgeable about housing subsidy programs, helped the community group develop a proposal, in partnership with a local developer, that they submitted to the state housing finance agency. The proposal requested funds to subsidize construction costs and a below-market-rate mortgage to finance a new housing development. The social worker did not disclose to his clients or the housing finance agency staff that he was a part-time consultant to the local developer who was a partner in the project and that he would benefit financially if the project were funded.

- A social worker was hired by a nursing home as a consultant. The purpose of the consultation was to conduct a study assessing the adequacy of the nursing home's social services and recommend ways to improve staffing and services delivery. The consultant's final report offered a number of recommendations, including a recommendation that the nursing home consider developing a partnership with a nationally prominent, for-profit home health care agency. The social worker did not disclose that her sister was a partner in the home health care agency and, as a result, she could have an incentive to encourage the nursing home to contract with that agency.

- A social worker served as an assistant director of a county child welfare department. He was primarily responsible for the department's services related to child abuse and neglect (conducting investigations into suspected abuse and neglect; arranging and supervising foster care; and providing preventive, crisis intervention, and counseling services to families). The department received a report that a child placed in one of the department's foster homes had been sexually abused by the foster father. The social worker arranged for and supervised an investigation into the allegation, but the foster father was once a very close friend of the social worker, thus making it difficult for the social worker to be entirely objective.

- A professor of social work maintained a small private practice. One of this social worker's clients, an accountant, decided to make a career change and obtain an MSW, largely because of her successful experience in therapy. The client applied for admission to the local school of social work. The professor, who continued to function as the client's therapist, served on the school's admissions committee and received the client's application for review. She explained to the school's dean that she should not review the application because of a possible conflict of interest, although she did not disclose how she knew the applicant.

- A social worker was retained by a local family services agency to conduct a formal evaluation of the agency's family reunification program, which had the goal of strengthening families when a child had been placed in out-of-home care because of abuse or neglect. With the agency's assistance and cooperation, the social worker designed and conducted an ambitious study of the agency's staff, services, and client outcome. The final report included a number of recommendations for staff to consider.

Shortly before the project was concluded, the social worker was appointed to the board of a major foundation that had received a proposal from the same family services agency. The foundation staff asked the social worker to review the agency's proposal and recommend whether foundation funding should be approved. The social worker told his foundation colleagues about his prior involvement with the agency and recused himself from the review of the proposal.

Each of these cases requires special efforts to avoid actual or potential conflicts of interest. In the first example, the community organizer who was assisting the neighborhood group with a proposal to develop affordable housing for elderly residents should have disclosed to his colleagues and the staff of the housing finance agency that he was a part-time consultant to the developer involved in the project. He also could have considered drawing on the expertise of another developer with whom he was not affiliated. In the second case, the social worker who was a consultant to a nursing home should not have recommended formation of a partnership with a home health care agency in which her sister was a partner, because such a relationship could be personally beneficial to the social worker's sister but might not be in the nursing home's best interest. She should have disclosed her sister's involvement with the home health care agency to nursing home administrators. In the third example, the social worker in the child welfare department should have removed himself from any involvement in the investigation involving his former friend. He should have explained to colleagues and administrators that it would be inappropriate for him to have any involvement in the case. The fourth case illustrates how the social work professor appropriately explained to the school's dean that she knew the applicant from the community, and therefore it would not be appropriate for her to review the application and make a recommendation (to protect the client's privacy, the social worker should not disclose that the applicant was a client in her practice). The last example shows how the social worker retained by the family services agency to evaluate its program appropriately explained to his colleagues at the foundation the ways in which he was actively involved with the agency and recused himself from further review of the proposal submitted to the foundation.

STANDARD 1.06(b)

Social workers should not take unfair advantage of any professional relationship or exploit others to further their personal, religious, political, or business interests.

In some, but not all, cases, conflicts of interest arise because social workers are in a position to take advantage of their relationships with clients, as in the case of the prison-based social worker who referred clients to his community-based practice, the social worker who helped a community group draft a proposal for an affordable housing project for the elderly population, and the social worker who consulted with the nursing home in the examples described above. Practitioners need to be particularly careful to avoid exploiting their relationships with clients to further their personal, religious, political, or business interests (or the interests of people close to the social workers). Personal interests involve social workers' own mental health, social, and intimacy needs. For example, a social worker in private practice was counseling a young woman who sought help in addressing marital problems. After a time, the social worker realized that he was attracted to his client. Although the client's clinical needs had been met after 11 counseling sessions, the social worker encouraged her to stay in treatment longer. The social worker eventually disclosed his feelings to the client and explained that he encouraged her to remain in therapy so that he could continue having contact with her. Their relationship deteriorated, and the client filed an ethics complaint with the state licensing board, alleging that the social worker exploited their relationship, at considerable emotional and financial cost to her, to meet his own personal needs.

Religious interests involve the social worker's spiritual or faith needs. Social workers who have strong religious beliefs and convictions may inappropriately introduce religious content into their work with clients who did not ask for or consent to such an approach. Introducing religious content into social work interventions is not, by definition, unethical. A number of social work services are provided under explicitly religious auspices. In such cases, clients understand that the social services are being sponsored by religious organizations or individuals who integrate religion and counseling. This is not unethical as long as clients fully understand the nature of the services they receive, are informed of available alternatives, and consent to such an approach.

Ethical problems arise, however, when social workers use their position of authority to incorporate religious content into their social work without explicitly addressing this issue with clients, who may be vulnerable and susceptible to the social worker's religious influence. For example, a social worker employed by a state psychiatric hospital had very strong religious beliefs and felt obligated to acquaint patients with relevant biblical passages during counseling sessions. On one occasion a colleague accidentally walked into a meeting room where the social worker was kneeling and praying with a patient. The patient later complained to hospital officials about the social worker's emphasis on religion.

Political interests involve social workers' personal political or ideological agendas. Although it is certainly legitimate (and often essential) for social workers to have strong political beliefs, particularly as they pertain to social work's mission and value base, practitioners should not take unfair advantage of their relationships with clients to advance a political agenda.

Not all political activity involving clients is unethical. For example, many social workers and social services agencies actively encourage clients to register to vote. Generally speaking, however, social workers should not take advantage of their relationships with clients to encourage, exhort, or pressure them to support a political agenda that is congruent with their own. For example, a social worker in a community mental health agency who is pro-choice on the abortion issue should not lobby clients to write letters to state legislators opposing a pending bill that would limit women's legal reproductive options. Because of the social worker's position of authority in a client's life, clients who disagree with the social worker's position on the issue may feel pressured to comply with the request just to please the social worker. Similarly, a social worker who supports a particular candidate for public office should not recruit clients to work on or donate their own money to the campaign. Vulnerable clients may find it difficult to say no.

Finally, a social worker's business interests include entrepreneurial or other investment or financial activities in which he or she is involved. A social worker in private practice was a partner in a small restaurant in his community. During one period the social worker and his partner in the restaurant business encountered serious cash flow problems and were having difficulty paying their bills. One of the social worker's clients was a loan officer at a bank. The social worker approached the client about the possibility of obtaining a short-term loan while he and his partner reorganized the restaurant business. Clearly, the social worker was taking unfair advantage of his professional relationship with the client to further his own business interests.

STANDARD 1.06(c)

Social workers should not engage in dual or multiple relationships with clients or former clients in which there is a risk of exploitation or potential harm to the client. In instances when dual or multiple relationships are unavoidable, social workers should take steps to protect clients and are responsible for setting clear, appropriate, and culturally sensitive boundaries. (Dual or multiple relationships occur when social workers relate to clients in more than one relationship, whether professional, social, or business. Dual or multiple relationships can occur simultaneously or consecutively.)

For decades social workers have been aware of the need to maintain clear boundaries in their relationships with clients. Practitioners have understood that they should not be sexually involved or maintain intense social relationships with current clients. In recent years, however, social workers, as well as other groups of professionals, have developed a keener understanding of the many subtle issues that can arise in their relationships with clients. The concept of dual and multiple relationships conveys this richer understanding of the complex ways in which boundary issues can emerge in professional–client relationships.

Dual or multiple relationships can assume many forms, not all of which are ethically problematic. At one extreme are dual and multiple relationships that are not typically problematic, for example, when a social worker and client coincidentally attend the same play and have adjacent seats. The boundary issues are temporary and, most likely, manageable. There may be awkward moments, particularly when the client meets the social worker's spouse or partner during intermission, but this kind of unanticipated boundary issue may not unleash complex issues in the therapeutic relationship. This is not to say that an unanticipated social contact should be ignored—it may be useful to address the client's feelings about the encounter. However, in the long run this is not the kind of dual relationship that is likely to have harmful, long-standing consequences. These circumstances involve boundary crossings rather than egregious boundary violations (Gutheil & Gabbard, 1993; Reamer, 2001c, 2003a). They may involve social workers' efforts to be helpful to clients or they may involve unavoidable or unanticipated dual relationships. Below are several other examples of dual or multiple relationships that are not likely to be ethically problematic:

- A social worker's client and her nine-year-old daughter canvassed their neighborhood to sell wrapping paper as a fundraiser for the daughter's school. The client was not aware that her social worker, with whom she was in psychotherapy, lived in the neighborhood, and she was surprised to discover that the social worker lived in one of the houses her daughter approached. The social worker purchased some wrapping paper from the client's daughter.

- A school social worker provided counseling services to an 11-year-old student and his parents. The student was referred to the social worker because a teacher was concerned about a sudden deterioration in his school work. Shortly after they began their work together, the social worker and the student's father realized that they were enrolled together in a continuing education class on computer technology.
- A social worker retained to evaluate a local family services agency's substance abuse program discovered that she and the program director were members of the same fitness center. Afterward, the social worker and the program director usually encountered each other once or twice a week at the center.

In each of these situations, it may be appropriate for the social workers to talk with their clients about their encounters outside the professional–client relationship to ensure that the encounters will not interfere with or undermine their work together. In all likelihood, superficial contact of this sort will not introduce difficult issues in the professional–client relationship.

At the other extreme are dual or multiple relationships that are clearly problematic, as in these examples that involve more intimate, self-serving, and exploitative circumstances:

- A social worker in a residential treatment program for adolescents met regularly with the single mother of a 12-year-old client. The social worker realized that he was attracted to the client's mother and began dating her.
- A clinical social worker had provided counseling to a man who reported that he was dealing with a midlife crisis and possible career change. Counseling ended after 10 months of what both parties regarded as a very successful therapeutic relationship. Three weeks after the termination of the professional–client relationship, the former client telephoned to invite the social worker to become a financial partner in the former client's new business venture. The social worker accepted the very attractive offer.
- A clinical social worker in an outpatient substance abuse treatment program for adults provided counseling to a young man who was struggling with alcohol abuse. As part of the counseling, the social worker encouraged the client to attend Alcoholics Anonymous (AA) meetings in the community. The social worker also was a recovering alcoholic. The social worker regularly attended AA meetings and invited the client to accompany her to meetings. The social worker and client attended meetings regularly, during which the social worker often disclosed personal information about her own recovery and substance abuse history.

In these cases the dual or multiple relationships are clearly problematic because of the likelihood of exploitation of or potential harm to the client. The social worker who dated his client's mother was involved in a dual relationship that could be very harmful to the client. The relationship with the client's mother could certainly undermine the client's trust in the social worker and confuse the client about the social worker's role in his life. The social worker's clinical judgment also could be impaired because of his intimate relationship with the client's mother.

The therapist who accepted her former client's offer to invest in his new business venture entered into a dual relationship that could be very detrimental to the former client. Dealing with the former client in a new relationship that focused on business and financial decisions could subvert the effectiveness of the former—and very recent—therapeutic relationship, particularly if contentious issues or disagreements were to arise. Over time the former client's perception of and feelings about the social worker might change because of the business relationship, and this could have a detrimental effect on whatever beneficial outcomes were achieved during the course of the professional–client relationship.

The social worker who was in recovery and attended AA meetings with her client could harm him as a result of the confused boundary issues. The client might have difficulty distinguishing between the social worker as a professional and the social worker as an acquaintance who is also in recovery. This confusion could interfere with the social worker's professional effectiveness and with the client's recovery.

What these cases have in common is risk of harm to the client. As Kagle and Giebelhausen (1994) observed with respect to the psychotherapeutic relationship,

> Dual relationships involve boundary violations. They cross the line between the therapeutic relationship and a second relationship, undermining the distinctive nature of the therapeutic relationship, blurring the roles of practitioner and client, and permitting the abuse of power. In a therapeutic relationship, the practitioner's influence on the client is constrained by professional ethics and other protocols of professional practice. When a professional relationship shifts to a dual relationship, the practitioner's power remains but is not checked by the rules of professional conduct or, in some cases, even acknowledged. The practitioner and the client pretend to define the second relationship around different roles and rules. Behavior that is incompatible with a therapeutic relationship is made to seem acceptable in the context of the second relationship. Attention shifts from the client to the practitioner, and power appears to be more equally shared. (p. 217)

Not surprisingly, in between these extremes of dual and multiple relationships are "gray areas" where the boundary issues are unclear. In such circumstances reasonable social workers may disagree about the degree of risk for potential harm or exploitation. For example,

• A social worker for a substance abuse treatment program worked with a 28-year-old woman who had a history of cocaine and alcohol abuse. The client claimed that, as a result of her work with the social worker, she was "clean and sober" for the first time in her adult life, employed, and in a solid relationship. The social worker received an invitation from the client to attend her upcoming wedding. The client told the social worker how important it was for her to attend the wedding in light of the social worker's major influence in the client's life. The social worker was uncertain about whether to attend the wedding; she did not want the client to feel rejected, but she was uneasy about blurring the boundaries in their relationship.

• A social worker employed by a home health care agency provided services to a terminally ill 72-year-old woman who was receiving hospice services. The social worker visited once each week to provide counseling and support. During one of the visits, the client invited the social worker to join her for lunch. The social worker was torn between politely rejecting the invitation to avoid blurring the boundaries in the relationship and accepting the invitation to avoid hurting the client's feelings and, perhaps, jeopardizing the clinical relationship.

- A social worker in private practice in a rural area provided counseling services to a 32-year-old man who was struggling with self-esteem issues. Three years after the professional–client relationship ended, and primarily as a result of the client's contact with the social worker, the client enrolled in a nearby graduate program in social work. After his graduation, which was six years after the termination of the professional–client relationship, the former client approached the social worker about providing him with clinical supervision. The former client explained that he wanted to learn from the social worker's vast experience and that in their area there were no other MSWs available to provide clinical supervision. The social worker believed that he could manage this new relationship with his former client, especially because several years had elapsed since the termination of the professional–client relationship, but he was unsure this change in roles was appropriate.

- A school social worker received a substantial restaurant gift certificate at the end of the school year from the family of a low-income student. The parents explained that the gift was their way of thanking the social worker for all the help she provided during the course of the year. The social worker was unsure about whether to accept the gift.

When faced with such circumstances, social workers should consult with experienced colleagues and supervisors to think through their decisions thoroughly and responsibly. Social workers also should document that they obtained such consultation and supervision to demonstrate that they made a diligent effort to handle the situation ethically. Social workers should also review relevant regulations and agency policies. In some cases there may not be an obvious "right" answer; however, competent consultation and supervision are essential to minimize the likelihood that clients will be harmed by social workers' decisions to enter into a dual or multiple relationship with a client or former client.

Social workers also should recognize that some dual and multiple relationships are more avoidable than others. For example, they can easily avoid planned social encounters with their clients, such as spending a day together at the beach or going out to dinner. In contrast, it may be difficult for social workers to avoid dual or multiple relationships in small or rural communities where, for example, a former client may marry her social worker's closest friend in town, a current client is elected to the local court in which the social worker's spouse frequently practices, or a social worker and her client are both appointed to the board of their community church.

In such circumstances, according to Standard 1.06(c), social workers must "take steps to protect clients and are responsible for setting clear, appropriate, and culturally sensitive boundaries." At a minimum, social workers should discuss the boundary issues frankly with their clients; in addition, they should consult colleagues and supervisors to discuss the most appropriate ways to handle boundary issues that have emerged (for example, referring the client to a colleague to avoid a problematic dual relationship).

When faced with actual or potential dual or multiple relationships, social workers should critically examine their own motives and needs, which they previously may have failed to do (Reamer, 2001c). In many cases involving inappropriate and harmful dual and multiple relationships, social workers are motivated more by self-gratification and their own emotional needs than by a genuine, primary, and deep-seated commitment to the client's needs. Social workers also may find that they are more impulsive in these relationships than in other areas of their lives, because they have placed their own needs above those of their clients. In addition, social workers involved in problematic dual or multiple relationships may find that they have difficulty empathizing with clients—again, because of their preoccupation with their own needs rather than those of their clients.

STANDARD 1.06(d)

When social workers provide services to two or more people who have a relationship with each other (for example, couples, family members), social workers should clarify with all parties which individuals will be considered clients and the nature of social workers' professional obligations to the various individuals who are receiving services. Social workers who anticipate a conflict of interest among the individuals receiving services or who anticipate having to perform in potentially conflicting roles (for example, when a social worker is asked to testify in a child custody dispute or divorce proceedings involving clients) should clarify their role with the parties involved and take appropriate action to minimize any conflict of interest.

Clinical social workers often provide services to two or more people who have a relationship with each other. Common examples include family, marital, or couples therapy; discharge planning for a hospital patient that includes family consultation; case management for elderly clients and their families; and school social work that requires parental involvement. Social workers often provide such services without encountering a potential or actual conflict of interest. However, circumstances sometimes arise in which a serious conflict of interest occurs or might occur:

- A clinical social worker provided individual counseling to a 34-year-old woman who was distressed about her nine-year-old son's behavioral problems. After initially focusing on the child's behavioral issues and strategies for dealing with them, the client brought up some problems related to her marriage. Soon it became clear that the marital issues were contributing to the child's behavioral problems. At first the client's husband was unwilling to participate in the therapy, but eventually, as the marriage deteriorated, he agreed to participate.

  Ultimately, the couple decided to divorce and became involved in a bitter child custody dispute. The husband's lawyer subpoenaed the social worker to testify against the mother about a number of issues related to the child custody dispute.

- A hospital social worker provided services to an 82-year-old woman who was recovering from hip surgery. In addition to her physical problems, the patient also manifested some symptoms of dementia (some modest difficulty learning new information and remembering learned information, performing motor functions, recognizing familiar objects). The client's son, who visited his mother regularly, insisted that the social worker attempt to place his mother in a nursing home. He was very concerned about his mother's dementia symptoms and the risks she faced if she returned to her home to live alone. The client, however, adamantly refused to go to a nursing home and insisted that the social worker arrange home health care; the client said she was willing to assume any risk associated with her living alone.

● A school social worker began counseling a 13-year-old student who was referred by the student's guidance counselor. According to the guidance counselor, the student seemed to be depressed. The social worker and the student met weekly for about two months. With the student's permission, the social worker also met with his parents several times to gather background information about the family's history and relationships and explore the parents' perceptions of their son's difficulties. One afternoon the student's mother telephoned the social worker and asked for an update on his situation at school, but the student was concerned about his privacy and had asked the social worker not to disclose to his parents any information from their counseling sessions.

When social workers provide services to two or more people who have a relationship with each other, they must always think ahead about possible conflicts of interest. Early in any such relationship, social workers should discuss with the parties involved which individuals will be considered clients and the various commitments and obligations the social worker has to all parties involved. For example, social workers who provide marriage or couples counseling should routinely bring up the subject of potential conflicts of interest so that the participants clearly understand the social worker's role and the social worker's effort not to take sides with one person or another. This explanation would not necessarily prevent one party's lawyer from subpoenaing a social worker in a divorce proceeding or custody dispute, but the clients would be fully aware of possible conflicts of interest when they enter their clinical relationship with the social worker.

Similarly, social workers who depend on collateral contacts with family members (or other third parties) to serve their primary clients (for example, social workers in hospitals or schools) should clarify with all parties which individuals will be considered clients and the nature of the social worker's obligations to the various individuals involved. For instance, the hospital social worker in the example above should inform the elderly patient's son and the patient about her primary commitment to the patient, her obligation to respect the patient's right to self-determination, and her simultaneous obligation to take reasonable steps to protect the patient from self-harm. This explanation may not be entirely satisfactory to the son, but it can clarify the social worker's principal obligations and manage potentially conflicting interests as the situation unfolds. The school social worker discussed above should explain to the student and his parents the nature of the social worker's relationship with the student and his policy regarding confidentiality (and the reasons for it). The parents may not agree with this policy, but such an explanation may help manage the parties' diverse agendas and avoid potential conflicts of interest.

Privacy and Confidentiality

STANDARD 1.07(a)

Social workers should respect clients' right to privacy. Social workers should not solicit private information from clients unless it is essential to providing services

or conducting social work evaluation or research. Once private information is
shared, standards of confidentiality apply.

Social workers often have access to sensitive information about intimate aspects
of clients' lives, including information about personal relationships, domestic violence,
substance abuse, sexual trauma and behavior, criminal activity, and mental illness. Such
information is obtained to assess clients' circumstances thoroughly, so that social workers can plan and implement appropriate interventions.

Social workers should be conservative, however, in their efforts to obtain private
information from clients. That is, they should seek private information from clients only
to the extent that it is necessary to carry out their professional functions. Social workers
should constantly distinguish between private information that is essential and private
information that is gratuitous. For example, a social worker employed by a residential
substance abuse treatment program would have good reasons for asking new clients
about their abuse of alcohol, cocaine, amphetamines, and other drugs. However, it
would not be appropriate for that social worker to ask invasive questions about clients'
sexual orientation. A client may wish to bring this subject up if it is somehow related to
his or her substance abuse problems, but the social worker should follow the client's lead
and respect that person's right to privacy.

Similarly, a social worker in a community mental health center should not routinely ask clients about past criminal activity in which they may have engaged that has
no direct bearing on their current circumstances. In this setting, social workers may be
tempted to ask clients about their past conduct, but unless there is some legally sanctioned mandate or compelling clinical reason to gather such information, they should
respect their clients' privacy.

When clients voluntarily share private information or when it is appropriate for
social workers to ask for private information to provide services or conduct research,
client confidentiality must be protected. The *NASW Code of Ethics* includes a number of
standards designed to protect client confidentiality to the greatest extent possible.

STANDARD 1.07(b)

Social workers may disclose confidential information when appropriate with
valid consent from a client or a person legally authorized to consent on behalf
of a client.

There are two kinds of situations in which social workers are in a position to disclose confidential information. First, clients may ask social workers to release confidential information to a third party. For example, a client may ask a social worker to disclose confidential information to another services provider, such as a physician or
therapist, or to a lawyer who is representing the client in a legal matter, such as a child
custody dispute or a lawsuit the client's lawyer filed on the client's behalf against another
professional who provided services to the client. Second, social workers may receive
requests for confidential information from third parties. For example, a social worker
may receive a request for confidential information from law enforcement officials who
are investigating a crime that involved the social worker's client, from a nursing home

to which the client has been admitted, or from a lawyer who is defending a party whom the client has sued.

In these situations, social workers should disclose confidential information only when they have obtained valid consent from the client or a person legally authorized to consent on behalf of the client. (There are several exceptions to this mandate, particularly ones involving emergency circumstances and court orders to disclose confidential information, which are discussed in Standard 1.07[c].) The consent obtained from a client, or a person legally authorized to consent on the client's behalf (such as a relative or friend who has a power of attorney), should conform to the informed-consent standards set forth in Standards 1.03(a), (b), and (c). That is, in obtaining client consent to disclose confidential information, social workers should use clear and understandable language to inform clients of the purpose of the consent and the disclosure, the risks related to the disclosure, reasonable alternatives (if any), the client's right to refuse or withdraw consent, and the time frame covered by the consent. Social workers also should provide clients with an opportunity to ask questions about the consent to disclose confidential information.

As with any informed-consent procedure, when social workers seek client consent to disclose confidential information they must take special precautions when a client is not literate or has difficulty understanding the primary language used in the practice setting (see Standard 1.03[b]). Social workers may need to provide such clients with a detailed oral explanation or arrange for a qualified interpreter or translator. If clients lack the capacity to provide informed consent to the disclosure of confidential information, social workers should protect clients' interests to the greatest extent possible by seeking permission from an appropriate third party, informing clients consistent with their level of understanding and comprehension, and attempting to ensure that the third party acts in a manner consistent with the client's wishes and interests (see Standard 1.03[c]). Particular care should be taken to ensure that clients do not feel coerced or pressured into consenting to the disclosure.

Many requests for confidential information received by social workers are straightforward. For example, another professional providing services to a client may request confidential information concerning that client; the social worker and the client should discuss the request and consent procedure before the client signs the consent form and the information is shared with the requesting party.

In other cases, however, social workers may be less clear about the appropriateness of a request for disclosure of confidential information. One source of confusion is the extent to which the party requesting the confidential information is legally entitled to it (for example, whether parents are entitled to confidential information concerning their children or whether law enforcement officials are entitled to confidential information about one's client). In such circumstances, social workers should consult with knowledgeable colleagues—and, if necessary, a lawyer—about relevant statutes and regulations.

A second source of confusion involves situations in which a social worker questions a client's decision to consent to disclosure of confidential information. For example, a social worker in private practice was asked by her client to disclose confidential information concerning his therapy to the client's employer. The employer had asked the client for this information for reassurance that the client was addressing a mental health problem that affected his job performance. The social worker was concerned about disclosing the amount of information requested by the employer; in her judgment, some of the information in her case notes might be used against the client. Although the social worker shared her concern with the client, the client continued to insist that all the information be shared with the employer. Thus, when social workers believe that complying with a client's request to disclose confidential information would not be in the client's best interest, they should discuss the concerns with the client. If the client continues to insist on the disclosure, social workers should comply with the client's wishes; however, practitioners should document that they discussed the issue with the client. Such documentation helps protect a social worker if questions should subsequently be raised about the appropriateness of the disclosure. As in all cases in which social workers are uncertain about how best to proceed, they should consult with knowledgeable colleagues or a lawyer.

There are a number of substantive areas where social workers should clarify when client consent is and is not required for disclosure of confidential information. Numerous authors have discussed these situations, which may be governed by federal, state, or local laws or regulations (Austin et al., 1990; Dickson, 1995, 1998; Madden, 2003; Reamer, 2003b; Stein, 2004). They include the disclosure of confidential information pertaining to

- protection of third parties and clients who may be at risk (see Standard 1.07[c])
- assessment, treatment, or referral of clients to address substance abuse issues
- mandatory reporting of suspected abuse or neglect of a child, senior citizen, or person with disabilities
- coordination of services with other agencies involved with clients (for example, public welfare agencies, psychiatric facilities, school officials)
- the delivery of services within one's own agency (the extent to which staff within an agency should share confidential information with one another)
- peer supervision and consultation with colleagues (see Standard 2.05 [c])
- deceased clients (see Standard 1.07[r])
- news media (see Standard 1.07[k])
- law enforcement officials
- minors' parents or guardians
- court orders.

STANDARD 1.07(c)

Social workers should protect the confidentiality of all information obtained in the course of professional service, except for compelling professional reasons. The general expectation that social workers will keep information confidential does not apply when disclosure is necessary to prevent serious, foreseeable, and imminent harm to a client or other identifiable person. In all instances, social workers should disclose the least amount of confidential information necessary to achieve the desired purpose; only information that is directly relevant to the purpose for which the disclosure is made should be revealed.

The concept of disclosing confidential information contrary to a client's wishes has been considered in the discussion of Standard 1.02, which concerns the limits of clients' right to self-determination. Standard 1.02 explicitly acknowledges that circumstances may arise in which social workers are obligated to limit a client's right to self-determination—specifically when, in the social worker's judgment, a client's actions or potential actions pose a serious, foreseeable, and imminent risk to himself or herself or to others.

As discussed under Standard 1.02, the *Tarasoff* (1976) case established the most noteworthy precedent concerning the disclosure of confidential information to protect third parties from harm. Since the *Tarasoff* decision, many court cases involving duty-to-protect issues have been litigated, further clarifying social workers' and other mental health professionals' obligations. In addition, in recent years many states have adopted statutes incorporating the guidelines established in *Tarasoff* and other duty-to-warn and duty-to-protect cases (Kopels & Kagle, 1993; Lewis, 1986; Reamer, 2003b). Although some court rulings are contradictory or inconsistent, and there is some variation among state statutes, the general trend suggests that, ordinarily, four conditions should be met to justify disclosure of confidential information to protect a third party from harm. First, the social worker should have evidence that the client poses a threat of violence to a third party. As the court asserted in *Tarasoff*, "when a therapist determines, or pursuant to the standards of his profession should determine, that his patient presents a serious danger of violence to another, he incurs an obligation to use reasonable care to protect the intended victim against such danger" (17 Cal. 3d 425 at 431). Although courts have not provided precise definitions of *violence*, the term ordinarily implies the use of some kind of force (for example, using a gun, knife, or other dangerous weapon) to inflict harm.

Second, the social worker should have evidence that the violent act is foreseeable—that is, sufficient evidence to suggest that the violent act is likely to occur. Although courts recognize that social workers and other mental health professionals cannot predict violence with absolute certainty, clinicians must be able to demonstrate that they had reason to believe that the client was likely to carry out the violent act (based, for example, on the client's behavior and comments).

Third, the social worker should have reasonable evidence to suggest that the violent act is impending or likely to occur relatively soon. Here, too, the courts have not provided precise criteria or guidelines. *Imminence* may be defined differently by different clinicians; ultimately, the social worker should be able to defend his or her definition, whether it is in terms of minutes, hours, or days.

Fourth, a number of court decisions, but not all, require that a clinician be able to identify the potential victim. The rationale is that the disclosure of confidential information against a client's wishes should be exceptional and should not occur unless the clinician has very specific information about the client's apparent intent to harm a specific probable victim (Lewis, 1986). It also is possible that a duty to protect would exist if a social worker can infer the identity of a foreseeable victim from information available in a case, even if the client has not specifically named the probable victim (Austin et al., 1990; Reamer, 2003b).

Although these criteria are fairly straightforward, social workers should be aware that both clinicians and lawyers disagree about their application and "goodness of fit" in individual cases. Most agree that a social worker whose client makes a clear threat to violently harm an identifiable third party within the next day or so has a duty to take steps to protect the potential victim, which may entail disclosing confidential information without the client's consent.

Other cases, however, are not so clear. For example, a social worker at an outpatient mental health clinic was providing clinical services to a young man who had been discharged from a psychiatric hospital after treatment for bipolar disorder. The client was functioning well in the community and complying with his medication regimen; he was employed and involved in a relationship with a woman he had met at work. The client met with the social worker every two weeks.

One afternoon the client telephoned the social worker and said he needed to see her "as soon as possible to discuss some terrible news." The next morning at the social worker's office, the client informed her that, much to his surprise, he was just diagnosed with HIV infection, the virus that causes AIDS. The client explained to the social worker that he had never thought he was in a high-risk category, although he acknowledged that about four years earlier he had been involved in a brief sexual relationship with another man. The social worker and client extensively discussed the implications of the HIV diagnosis, particularly with respect to the client' lifestyle and his relationship with his girlfriend. The social worker soon discovered that the client had not shared with his partner the fact that he had been diagnosed with HIV. The client told the social worker, "She's the best thing that's happened to me in my adult life. My head tells me I should tell her, but my heart is so afraid. I can't bear the thought that I might lose her. But you don't need to worry—the nurse at the health clinic told me how to prevent HIV transmission." The client then described to the social worker all of the precautions he would take to protect his partner, "who I love so very much." He went on to say, "One of these days, I'll get the courage to tell her. I just can't do it now. I'm emotionally paralyzed. Please, please don't say anything to her. You know I wouldn't do anything to harm her."

The social worker discussed the case with her supervisor and several colleagues and tried various clinical interventions to help the client get to a point where he would be willing to share with his partner the news of his HIV diagnosis (offering to role play the conversation with the client's girlfriend, offering to sit in on the actual conversation). Unfortunately, this clinical strategy was not successful. The social worker had to decide whether to honor the client's request for privacy and confidentiality or to take steps to ensure that the client's partner had sufficient information to protect herself. This was especially difficult considering that the social worker's colleagues disagreed about the social worker's obligation.

Circumstances such as these have generated considerable disagreement among social workers and lawyers about the relevance of *Tarasoff* and various duty-to-protect guidelines that have evolved since that precedent-setting decision (Francis & Chin, 1987; Gray & Harding, 1988; Kain, 1988; Reamer, 1991a, 1991b). When the *Tarasoff* case was decided in 1976, no one anticipated its eventual application to AIDS-related cases, because that syndrome did not become well known until 1981. Since the *Tarasoff* decision, some human services professionals have argued that the fact that an HIV-positive individual merely poses a threat to another party is sufficient to rely on the *Tarasoff*-like criteria to protect third parties (Lamb, Clark, Drumheller, Frizzell, & Surrey, 1989). Others, however, claim that *Tarasoff* is not an appropriate precedent because people with HIV infection may not explicitly threaten a third party with an act of violence. In the case discussed above, the client never threatened to harm his partner; in fact, he proclaimed his love for her and his intent to protect her by taking precautions. Moreover, in many cases the risk to third parties may not be demonstrably imminent and a particular potential victim may not be identifiable.

The key point is that circumstances may arise in which social workers are unclear about the extent of their duty to protect third parties in light of prevailing case law and statutes. As Lewis (1986) concluded, "it must . . . be recognized that psychotherapy is an imperfect science. A precise formula for determining when the duty to maintain confidentiality should yield to the duty to warn is, therefore, beyond reach" (pp. 614–615).

Social workers also may be obligated to disclose confidential information when a client poses a threat to himself or herself (Madden, 2003; VandeCreek & Knapp, 1993). That is, they are obligated to take reasonable steps to prevent a client's suicide, and this may entail disclosing confidential information (for example, to family members or other mental health professionals who may be in a position to prevent a suicide attempt). As Meyer and colleagues (1988) noted,

> While the law generally does not hold anyone responsible for the acts of another, there are exceptions. One of these is the responsibility of therapists to prevent suicide and other self-destructive behavior by their clients. The duty of therapists to exercise adequate care and skill in diagnosing suicidality is well-established. . . . When the risk of self-injurious behavior is identified an additional duty to take adequate precautions arises. . . . When psychotherapists fail to meet these responsibilities, they may be held liable for injuries that result. (p. 38)

Specific laws and regulations may require social workers to disclose confidential information without a client's consent. Perhaps the most common are mandatory reporting laws pertaining to suspected abuse or neglect of a child, senior citizen, or disabled person. Especially since the widespread establishment in the 1960s and 1970s of statutes on mandatory reporting of child abuse and neglect, social workers have come to accept their responsibility to disclose confidential information in some exceptional circumstances.

Here too, however, social workers' ethical decisions are not always clear. Sometimes social workers may be reluctant to comply with a mandatory reporting statute because of their concern about jeopardizing their therapeutic relationship with a client; social workers in this situation may believe that they can manage the risk themselves. Practitioners who decide not to comply with mandatory reporting statutes should recognize that they assume considerable risk in the form of potential ethics complaints and lawsuits. Child welfare officials and other interested parties who become aware that a social worker had reason to suspect abuse or neglect and yet failed to report this concern may file an ethics complaint or lawsuit against the social worker. This could occur, for example, if the social worker's client subsequently neglects or abuses the party at risk and an investigation reveals that the social worker failed to report the suspected abuse or neglect.

An important element of Standard 1.07(c) is its requirement that, when social workers are obligated to disclose confidential information, they should disclose "the least amount of confidential information necessary to achieve the desired purpose; only information that is directly relevant to the purpose for which the disclosure is made should be revealed." Although extraordinary and compelling circumstances may require social workers to disclose confidential information, practitioners should be conservative about which and how much information is shared. Only information that is absolutely essential for the recipient to have (for example, to protect a third party from harm or to prevent a suicide) should be disclosed. Thus, if a client threatens to harm his estranged spouse, law enforcement officials notified by the social worker should be given the least information possible to enable the police to prevent harm (for example, the identity of the party at risk, the nature of the threat the client poses, recommendations for the most effective way to intervene with the client). It should not be necessary for the social worker to share extensive details of clinical history, particularly facts that are extraneous to the threat.

STANDARD 1.07(d)

Social workers should inform clients, to the extent possible, about the disclosure of confidential information and the potential consequences, when feasible before the disclosure is made. This applies whether social workers disclose confidential information on the basis of a legal requirement or client consent.

In those extraordinary circumstances that require social workers to disclose confidential information, they should attempt to inform clients about the disclosure before it is made. Common courtesy requires that clients be told when important information about them is going to be shared with others (such as child welfare officials, when a social worker suspects possible abuse or neglect, or law enforcement officials, when a social worker is concerned that a client is planning to harm a third party), especially when the disclosure will be made without the client's consent.

Also, informing clients about the disclosure may affect the circumstances that led to the need for the disclosure. In some but not all cases, clients who are reluctant to consent to the disclosure of information may change their minds when they learn that the social worker is serious about his or her decision to disclose confidential information. For example, a social worker in a home health care program was concerned that the son of her elderly client, a 79-year-old man diagnosed with Alzheimer's disease, was physically abusing his father. The son adamantly denied the abuse and warned the social worker not to share this information with anyone, "or there will be trouble you don't want to have." The son's threat added to the social worker's concern. She decided that she had to report her concern to the state department of elderly affairs, as required by law. She also decided that she would tell her client's son before she made the report. Once the social worker explained her concern and obligation to the son—as diplomatically as possible—the son began to cry and admitted that he had "lost control a few times." He then talked at length about "how unbearable it is to take care of someone with this disease." This clinical breakthrough enabled the social worker to provide genuine assistance and support to the son, who was then eager to learn about ways to cope with his situation and his father's disease. The social worker's informing the son of her plan to notify the department of elderly affairs was the catalyst needed to help him acknowledge his frustration and abusive behavior. Later the social worker and the son together called the department of elderly affairs and described their plan to address the son's frustration and coping mechanisms. The protective services worker at the department commended the son for his willingness to address the issues he was facing and approved the plan.

Note that Standard 1.07(d) states that clients should be informed about the disclosure of confidential information and the potential consequences "to the extent possible" and "when feasible" before the disclosure is made. The NASW Code of Ethics Revision Committee recognized that, in some circumstances, it may not be feasible or realistic to inform clients in advance—or at all—about the disclosure. For practical reasons under no one's control, it may not be possible to reach a client before a disclosure is made. For example, a social worker at a family services agency was telephoned by his client's wife, who also met with the social worker occasionally. According to the wife, her husband, with whom she had just had a serious fight, "just stormed out of the house with the children and said I'd never see them again, except at their funeral. The kids were screaming at the top of their lungs, they were so afraid. I know he's going to do something awful to them just to get back at me. He'll really do it." The husband had a history of violence, having physically abused both his wife and their children. After consulting with his supervisor, the social worker decided to notify local child welfare and law enforcement officials and discuss with them the most appropriate way to intervene to protect the children. This involved disclosing confidential information without notifying the client ahead of time. In the circumstances, it was not feasible to notify the client in advance.

It also may not be wise or possible to inform the client of the disclosure when the social worker would be at risk of harm. For example, in the case involving the son who had abused his father, it is conceivable that the social worker would have been physically afraid of the client, who had warned her not to talk to anyone about her concerns, "or there will be trouble you don't want to have." Such risk is difficult to assess, but situations can arise when social workers conclude, quite reasonably, that the physical risk they face from informing clients of the impending disclosure of confidential information is too great. Social workers should be careful to obtain proper consultation in such situations and document their concerns and rationale.

Not all decisions by social workers to disclose confidential information stem from a legal requirement such as an obligation to protect third parties from harm or to report suspected abuse or neglect of a child, senior citizen, or person with a disability. Often social workers disclose confidential information based on clients' consent, for example, when information is shared willingly with other services providers. In such cases, social workers should be sure that a client is informed about the timing of the disclosure, its purpose and content, the client's right to refuse or withdraw consent, the time frame covered by the consent, and any potential consequences (see Standard 1.03[a]). It is always wise to document that clients were given this information.

STANDARD 1.07(e)

Social workers should discuss with clients and other interested parties the nature of confidentiality and limitations of clients' right to confidentiality. Social workers should review with clients circumstances where confidential information may be requested and where disclosure of confidential information may be legally required. This discussion should occur as soon as possible in the social worker–client relationship and as needed throughout the course of the relationship.

Clients have the right to know how social workers will handle confidential information. Social workers have a responsibility to inform clients about their policies concerning confidentiality, particularly those related to any limitations. Social workers should draw on relevant statutes, regulations, and ethical standards of the profession when developing confidentiality policies.

Ideally, social workers should inform clients of their confidentiality policies early in the social worker–client relationship. In most cases this can occur during the first meeting with a client. There are some times, however, when this may not be practical— for example, when a new client is in a state of crisis or when the social worker provides services in an emergency. In these situations, social workers should inform clients of their confidentiality policies as soon as possible. Also, occasions arise during the course of their work with clients when it is appropriate to reacquaint them with confidentiality policies (for example, when a social worker receives an unusual request for confidential information or is particularly concerned about protecting a third party from harm).

It is most often preferable for social workers to inform clients of their confidentiality policies both orally and in writing. A written summary of a social worker's confidentiality policies can help clients retain the information over time. Clients may be so overwhelmed during their first meeting with a social worker that they find it difficult to remember all the information that the social worker presented. In addition, a written summary signed by the client provides documentation that the social worker conveyed this information to the client.

A social worker's explanations of confidentiality policy should address a number of topics. Depending on the setting, these topics can include

- the importance of confidentiality in the social worker–client relationship (a brief statement of why the social worker treats the subject of confidentiality so seriously)
- laws, ethical standards, and regulations pertaining to confidentiality (relevant federal, state, and local laws and regulations; ethical standards in social work)
- measures that the social worker will take to protect clients' confidentiality (storing records in a secure location, limiting colleagues' and outside parties' access to records)
- circumstances in which the social worker would be obligated to disclose confidential information (for example, to comply with mandatory reporting laws or a court order, to protect a third party from harm or the client from self-injury)
- procedures that will be used to obtain clients' informed consent for the release of confidential information and any exceptions to this (a summary of the purpose and importance of and the steps involved in informed consent)
- procedures for sharing information with colleagues for consultation, supervision, and coordination of services (a summary of the roles of consultation, supervision, and coordination of services and why confidential information might be shared)
- access that third-party payers (insurers) or EAP staff will have to clients' records (social workers' policy for sharing information with managed care companies, insurance company representatives, utilization review personnel, and staff of EAPs)
- disclosure of confidential information by telephone, computer, fax machine, e-mail, and the Internet
- access to agency facilities and clients by outside parties (for example, people who come to the agency to attend meetings or participate in a tour)
- audiotaping and videotaping of clients.

STANDARD 1.07(f)

When social workers provide counseling services to families, couples, or groups, social workers should seek agreement among the parties involved concerning each individual's right to confidentiality and obligation to preserve the confidentiality of information shared by others. Social workers should inform participants in family, couples, or group counseling that social workers cannot guarantee that all participants will honor such agreements.

Social workers who provide counseling services to families, couples, or groups face special confidentiality issues. In addition to the usual exceptions to confidentiality found in individual counseling (such as social workers' obligation to disclose information in certain exceptional circumstances involving threats to harm third parties, prevention of suicide, and compliance with mandatory reporting laws and court orders), participants in family, couples, and group counseling also face the possibility that other participants will not respect the right to confidentiality. Social workers should inform clients that they cannot guarantee that other participants will not share information from family, couples, or group counseling with third parties.

Social workers who provide such clinical services have an obligation to seek agreement among the parties involved in counseling concerning each individual's right to confidentiality and the obligation to respect the confidentiality of information shared by others. Practitioners should consider preparing forms that explain the importance of confidentiality and request each participant's agreement to honor the others' right to confidentiality. For example, "I understand that confidentiality and privacy are basic to building trust among group members. I agree to keep confidential what other group members share, and I will not talk about what is shared during the group with others outside the group" (Houston-Vega & Nuehring, 1997, p. C-56; Reamer, 2003b, p. 270).

There is no consensus in the legal profession as to whether clients who disclose confidential information in the context of family, couples, or group counseling forfeit their right to have this confidentiality protected during legal proceedings (such as lawsuits involving personal injury or malpractice claims and custody or paternity disputes). Some lawyers argue that a client who discloses information to third parties in family, couples, or group counseling forfeits the right to have confidentiality protected because of his or her clear willingness to share this information with others. Others argue, however, that this sort of disclosure should not invalidate this right (Meyer et al., 1988).

Some courts have ruled that group therapy involves an expectation of privacy and that confidential information should be protected during legal proceedings (Meyer et al., 1988; Reamer, 2003b). In a case involving marital therapy, the Connecticut Appeals Court rejected the husband's argument that confidential information shared by the wife with the couple's therapist was not privileged and should have been disclosed in court. The husband had appealed the outcome of divorce and custody proceedings and wanted to introduce the therapist's testimony to support his arguments. He claimed that the disclosures made by his wife occurred during marital counseling rather than "psychological counseling" and therefore were not privileged. The appeals court held that the wife's communications were privileged and, because she had not waived the privilege, the therapist could not testify about her sessions with the wife or her sessions with the couple

("Psychologist–Patient Privilege," 1991). Because laws vary from state to state and case law is sometimes inconsistent, social workers should consult a lawyer to determine the current status in their state of clients' right to privileged communication in family, couples, and group counseling (Madden, 2003; VandeCreek, Knapp, & Herzog, 1988).

STANDARD 1.07(g)

Social workers should inform clients involved in family, couples, marital, or group counseling of the social worker's, employer's, and agency's policy concerning the social worker's disclosure of confidential information among the parties involved in the counseling.

Social workers who provide family, couples, marital, or group counseling should develop policies on sharing confidential information among the parties involved in the counseling. First, social workers who provide family, couples, or marital counseling need to clarify their policy (or their employer's or agency's policy) concerning the handling of "family secrets," particularly when a family member, a partner, or a spouse approaches the social worker to discuss an issue that he or she does not want shared with the others involved in the counseling. For example, a social worker who provided marital counseling to a couple received a telephone call from the husband, who requested an opportunity to meet with the social worker individually to discuss "a very personal matter that I don't feel comfortable discussing with my wife during counseling." It turned out that the husband was having an extramarital affair and wanted to discuss with the social worker how to end the affair. The social worker had to decide whether to meet with the husband individually and whether she would respect the husband's request for confidentiality.

Social workers' policies on this issue vary. Many practitioners, perhaps the majority, will not provide individual counseling to clients they are seeing in family, couples, or marital therapy because this can introduce clinical complexity (for example, problems related to confidentiality, the need for couples and family members to address their issues in therapy openly as a family or couple, or perceptions by clients that the social worker favors one party over another or is colluding with one party against another). These social workers explain to clients at the beginning of the therapeutic relationship that the family or couple is the client and they will not meet with the participants individually; any participant who wants individual counseling can ask for a referral to another practitioner. This may be accompanied by a statement that the social worker does not keep secrets and that it is important for the participants to be able to raise issues openly in the context of the counseling.

Some practitioners are willing to meet individually with participants in family, couples, or marital counseling sessions if—and only if—all the participants agree at the beginning of the counseling that this is an acceptable policy. Social workers who favor this approach typically explain that anyone who is seen individually will be regarded as a separate client with a separate case record and with an individual client's customary rights to confidentiality. That is, other participants in the family, couples, or group counseling will not have access to the case record involving the individual counseling, and any information shared within the context of the individual counseling will be considered confidential.

This is a complex and controversial issue. At present social workers disagree about the most appropriate way to handle requests for individual counseling made by participants in family, couples, or group counseling. In light of practitioners' different perspectives on the issue, they are, at the very least, obligated to explain to clients their policy (or their employer's or agency's policy) concerning the disclosure of confidential information among all parties involved in the counseling.

The second consideration concerning confidential information involves social workers who provide family counseling with minor children. As part of family counseling, social workers may spend time individually with a child. They should explain to clients how they will handle information shared by children during such individual counseling sessions. Many practitioners explain to family members, and especially to parents, that discussions they have with children in the parents' absence will be considered confidential, subject to the customary limitations (the obligation to disclose information if a child talks about harming himself or herself or others, in response to a court order, or to comply with a local law). Although the child will be encouraged to discuss his or her concerns in the context of family counseling, ordinarily the social worker will not share information disclosed during an individual counseling session. Parents who have legal custody, however, may have a legal right to inspect case records pertaining to their children unless there is compelling evidence that the children would be at risk of serious harm or the child is considered under the law to be a "mature" or "emancipated" minor.

Finally, social workers who provide group counseling typically have a firm policy that they will not talk individually with any group member about any other group member. This policy enhances trust among group members and avoids any perception of favoritism on the social worker's part or special alliances between the social worker and certain individual clients. There may be an occasional exception to this policy—for example, when a group counseling client also is receiving individual counseling from the social worker facilitating the group and the client feels the need to talk to the social worker about how to handle some troubling interpersonal dynamics in the group. Social workers are obligated to explain to group counseling participants how they handle such situations; under what, if any, circumstances other group members would be discussed in individual counseling sessions; and the extent to which this information would be considered confidential.

STANDARD 1.07(h)

Social workers should not disclose confidential information to third-party payers unless clients have authorized such disclosure.

Social workers routinely receive requests from third-party payers such as insurance and managed care companies for information about clients. Such information may include details of clients' mental health symptoms, psychiatric and other mental health treatment history, clinical diagnosis, and treatment plan. Ordinarily, third-party payers ask for this information to review requests for mental health and other social services for which clients may be eligible under their health insurance coverage.

Social workers should obtain clients' informed consent before disclosing confidential information to third-party payers. Consistent with Standards 1.03(a), (b), and (c), social workers should provide clients with a clear explanation of the purpose of the consent, risks related to it (for example, office staff who serve the third-party payer would have access to the confidential information), reasonable alternatives (for example, limiting the amount of detail shared with the third-party payer or bypassing the third-party payer entirely by paying for services out of pocket), clients' right to refuse or withdraw consent, and the time frame covered by the consent. Some social workers also include statements in the informed-consent form used for this purpose indicating that the client understands that the social worker cannot be responsible for the protection of the client's confidential information once it is shared with the third-party payer, and that the client releases the social worker from any liability connected with a breach of confidentiality by a third-party payer (sometimes called a *hold-harmless clause*).

STANDARD 1.07(i)

Social workers should not discuss confidential information in any setting unless privacy can be ensured. Social workers should not discuss confidential information in public or semipublic areas such as hallways, waiting rooms, elevators, and restaurants.

Ideally, social workers would discuss confidential information only in soundproofed settings where eavesdropping cannot occur. In reality, they sometimes find themselves in circumstances in which confidential information needs to be discussed, or it would be convenient to discuss, but there is a risk that the conversation would be overheard by others. This can occur, for example, when social workers suddenly and unexpectedly encounter in a hallway or elevator a colleague with whom they need to consult but have been unable to reach. It is understandable that the colleagues would want to take advantage of this opportunity to discuss pressing issues.

In one case, a relatively inexperienced social worker in a family services agency had been providing counseling to an adolescent who was using drugs. When the social worker learned that the client had made an unsuccessful suicide attempt, he was eager to consult with his supervisor, whom he had not been able to locate. The social worker unexpectedly encountered his supervisor in the agency's hallway, told her about the client's suicide attempt, and asked for advice about how best to proceed. Unbeknown to the social worker, another of the agency's clients, who knew the client from school, was sitting in a nearby office and overheard the entire conversation.

In some situations, social workers have control over privacy for their discussions of confidential information. With some effort, they can avoid discussing confidential information in agency hallways, waiting rooms, and elevators; in restaurants; at professional conferences; and so on. In other settings, however, it is difficult for social workers to protect the privacy of their discussions of confidential information. For example, some agencies do not provide social workers with individual or private offices. Staff may share an office or have unenclosed or only semipartitioned office space. Although social workers may not have the administrative authority to alter such architecture and office design, they should at least bring their concerns to the attention of appropriate administrators to have the issue addressed properly (see Standards 3.09[c] and [d]).

STANDARD 1.07(j)

Social workers should protect the confidentiality of clients during legal proceedings to the extent permitted by law. When a court of law or other legally authorized body orders social workers to disclose confidential or privileged information without a client's consent and such disclosure could cause harm to the client, social workers should request that the court withdraw the order or limit the order as narrowly as possible or maintain the records under seal, unavailable for public inspection.

There are many circumstances in which social workers may be asked or ordered to disclose confidential information, especially in the context of civil or criminal proceedings. Examples include social workers who are subpoenaed to testify in

- malpractice cases in which a client has sued another services provider (for example, a physician). The defendant's lawyer may subpoena the client's social worker to have him or her testify about comments the client made during counseling sessions. The defense lawyer may attempt to produce evidence that the lawsuit merely reflects the client's emotional instability, irrational tendencies, or vindictiveness; the defense also may try to show that the client has a history of mental health problems that preceded the mental health problems the client has alleged were caused by the defendant in the case. Defense lawyers may use this same strategy in other tort cases in which a social worker's client claims to have been wronged or injured by the actions of another party (for example, as a result of a workplace injury or automobile accident).
- divorce proceedings in which a social worker is subpoenaed by one spouse who believes that the social worker's testimony about confidential communications will support his or her claims against the other spouse.
- custody disputes in which one parent subpoenas a social worker who has worked with one or both parents, believing that the social worker's testimony will support his or her claim (for example, testimony concerning comments made during a counseling session about one parent's allegedly abusive behavior).
- paternity cases in which, for example, the child's birth mother subpoenas the putative father's social worker, believing that the social worker's testimony concerning the client's comments made during a counseling session about the couple's sexual relationship may support the birth mother's claim.
- criminal cases in which a prosecutor or defense attorney subpoenas a social worker to testify about the defendant's comments during counseling sessions.

Social workers may be asked to disclose confidential information during the discovery phase of a legal case or during the court hearing itself. Discovery is a pretrial procedure by which one party obtains information (facts and documents, for example) about the other. For example, during discovery a social worker may be asked to testify in a deposition under oath. In a deposition an attorney poses questions in the same form used in court. Depositions, or interrogatories, also may be taken in written form.

Social workers are obligated to protect clients' confidentiality during such legal proceedings to the extent permitted by law. To do so, they need to understand the concepts of privileged communication and subpoena. The concept of privilege concerns the admissibility of information in court, especially the extent to which courts may compel disclosure of confidential information during legal proceedings. The right of privileged communication—which assumes that a professional cannot disclose confidential information during legal proceedings without a client's consent—originated in British common law, under which no "gentleman" could be required to testify against another individual in court. Among professionals the attorney–client privilege was the first to be recognized, then the courts and various state legislatures eventually granted the right of privileged communication to clients of other groups of professionals, such as physicians, psychiatrists, psychologists, social workers, and clergy (Meyer et al., 1988; Reamer, 2003b; Stein, 2004; Wilson, 1978).

Many states have enacted legislation granting the right of privileged communication to social workers' clients during proceedings in state courts. Further, in the landmark case of *Jaffe v. Redmond* (1996), the U.S. Supreme Court ruled that clinical social workers and their clients have the right to privileged communication in federal courts as well (Alexander, 1997).

In general, courts insist that four conditions be met for information to be considered privileged (Wigmore, 1961):

1. The communication must originate in a confidence that it will not be disclosed;
2. The element of confidentiality must be essential to the full and satisfactory maintenance of the relationship between the parties;
3. The relation must be one which in the opinion of the community ought to be sedulously fostered; and
4. The injury that would inure to the relationship by the disclosure of the communication must be greater than the benefit thereby gained for the correct disposal of litigation. (p. 52)

Social workers who receive a subpoena to produce records or testify concerning confidential information should attempt to protect clients' confidentiality to the greatest extent possible. If the social worker is subpoenaed in a federal case or by a state court in a state that recognizes the social worker–client privilege, protecting client confidentiality may be easier.

Social workers must understand that it can be a mistake to disclose the information requested in a subpoena. Often social workers can legitimately argue that the requested information should not be disclosed (perhaps because the client has not provided consent or because of the damage this will cause to the social worker–client relationship) or can be obtained from some other source. A subpoena itself does not require a social worker to disclose information. Rather, a subpoena is a request for information, and the request may not be an appropriate one. Lawyers can issue subpoenas very easily, sometimes as a form of harassment, and may request the disclosure of information that they have no legal right to command (Grossman, 1978; Madden, 2003; Wilson, 1978).

Social workers who face subpoenas should follow several guidelines (Austin et al., 1990; Reamer, 2003b):

- Social workers should not release any information unless they are sure they have been authorized to do so (for example, in writing or in response to a court order).

- If it is unknown whether the privilege has been waived, social workers should claim the privilege to protect the client's confidentiality.
- If a social worker employs an assistant or trainee, the claim of privilege should extend to this individual, although the court might rule that unlicensed practitioners are not covered by the privilege.
- At a deposition, when no judge is present, social workers may have their own attorney present or choose to follow the advice and direction of the client's attorney.
- If a social worker's information about a client is embarrassing, damaging, or immaterial, written permission can be obtained to discuss the information with the client's attorney.
- Unless required to produce records or documents only (as with a subpoena duces tecum), social workers must appear at the location specified in the subpoena.
- If social workers are asked to appear in court to disclose confidential information and lack a signed release from the client, they should write a letter to the judge stating their wish to comply with the request but that the client has not waived the privilege. The court may or may not order disclosure of the information.

Several strategies can be used to protect clients' confidentiality during legal proceedings. If social workers believe that a subpoena is inappropriate (for example, because it requests information that should be considered privileged under state law), they can arrange for a lawyer (or perhaps the client's lawyer) to file a motion to quash the subpoena, which is an attempt to have the court rule that the request contained in the subpoena is inappropriate. A judge may issue a protective order explicitly limiting the disclosure of specific privileged information during the discovery phase of a case. In addition, social workers, perhaps through a lawyer, may request an in camera review (a review in the judge's chambers) of records or documents they believe should not be disclosed in open court. The judge can then decide whether the information should be revealed in open court and made a matter of public record.

STANDARD 1.07(k)

Social workers should protect the confidentiality of clients when responding to requests from members of the media.

There are various circumstances in which social workers might be asked for confidential information by members of the media (for example, newspaper, television, or radio reporters and staff):

- A newspaper reporter was investigating the arrest of a prominent elected official for domestic violence. A relative of the victim told the reporter that the official "has had a problem for a long time and has been in counseling" and mentioned the name of his social worker. The reporter contacted the social worker and asked her for information about the official's history of domestic violence.
- A television reporter was preparing a series on sexual abuse of children. The reporter contacted a local social worker who specialized in the treatment of perpetrators of childhood sexual abuse. During a recorded interview with the social worker, the

reporter asked the social worker to describe in detail the types of perpetrators with whom she had worked.

- A reporter for a national magazine was gathering information for an investigative report on neglect of nursing home residents. The reporter contacted the social worker at a prominent nursing home and asked him to describe cases of nursing home neglect he had witnessed.
- A nationally syndicated television talk show host and his staff were preparing a show on eating disorders. One of the show's producers contacted a social worker who specializes in the treatment of eating disorders and asked him to consider appearing on the show with one or two of his clients.

Social workers who are approached by members of the media must protect the confidentiality of their clients. If a reporter discovers that a person who is the subject of a story has been in treatment with a social worker and asks the social worker for specific information about the client, the social worker should respond by informing the reporter that, because of confidentiality requirements, he or she is not permitted to confirm or deny that the individual is or ever has been a client. If a social worker is asked by a reporter to talk about the types of clients she has worked with (for example, perpetrators of childhood sexual abuse), the social worker should speak only in very general terms, without disclosing any details or specific information that might enable the reporter or members of the public to identify individual clients.

Social workers may discuss specific clients or cases with the media only when clients have provided informed consent. In the example above, the elected official in treatment with a social worker to address domestic violence issues may want the social worker to talk somewhat openly with members of the media about the progress he has made to reassure the public during a political campaign. In the fourth example, the client may want to appear on a television talk show to discuss her clinical issues and may want the social worker to accompany her and participate in the discussion. In such exceptional circumstances, social workers must be especially careful to obtain truly informed consent. They should discuss with clients in detail the possible risks involved in having the social worker talk openly with members of the media (for example, the risk of public embarrassment or harassment or of undermining clinical progress) as well as possible benefits (for example, the possible therapeutic value of discussing one's issues openly, the opportunity to educate the public about an important issue).

STANDARD 1.07(l)

Social workers should protect the confidentiality of clients' written and electronic records and other sensitive information. Social workers should take reasonable steps to ensure that clients' records are stored in a secure location and that clients' records are not available to others who are not authorized to have access.

It is essential for social workers to ensure that clients' confidential written and electronic records are protected. This is especially important because of strict regulations in the federal Health Insurance Portability and Accountability Act of 1996 (P.L. 104-191), generally known as HIPAA (P.L. 104-191). There are several possible risks. With respect to written records, social workers should not leave case files in public or semipublic areas, available to people who are not authorized to have access to them. In agencies and offices, records should be stored in a secure location under lock and key.

- A clinical social worker in a community mental health center was scheduled to see five clients during the workday. He placed the clients' files on top of his desk at the beginning of the day, on the side closest to the chair in which clients typically sat. One of the clients glanced at the social worker's desk during the counseling session and read the names of the other clients that appeared in large letters on the tab of each case file.
- A clinical social worker in a group private practice was preparing a letter describing the progress a client was making in substance abuse counseling. The letter was to be sent to the client's employer, with the client's consent. At the end of the day the social worker had not finished the letter. She placed her notes in the case record and placed the record on top of her desk to remind her to resume work on the letter the following morning. Later that evening, a custodian entered the office to do his work. When the custodian picked up the wastepaper basket under the social worker's desk, he glanced at the desk and recognized the client's name on the outside of the case record. The client was the custodian's brother-in-law. The custodian then read the entire confidential case record.
- A clinical social worker in private practice in a large city took the commuter train home at the end of the day. The social worker took a client's case record with him so that he could review his notes that evening in preparation for a court hearing the following morning. During the long train ride, the social worker pulled out the case record and began reading it. He was unaware that the passenger next to him furtively read portions of the case notes.
- A social worker who was a case manager for an EAP took home two case records so she could finish some paper work. After dinner, she sat at the kitchen table to work on the project. Later that evening, she and her spouse went to a party. While the couple was out, the babysitter went to the kitchen for a snack, found the case records, and leafed through them.

As a general rule, social workers should not remove case records from the workplace (except, for example, when the case record must be brought to court in response to a court order or subpoena). Within the workplace, social workers should always place case records in a secure location, unavailable to people who do not have authorized access to them.

Social workers also need to be vigilant about the protection of clients' electronic records. Access to computer-based files must be restricted (for example, by secure passwords). In addition, social workers should take steps to ensure that confidential information displayed on computer monitors cannot be seen by members of the public or other unauthorized people. Monitors on administrative assistants' or social workers' desks, for example, should be positioned so that unauthorized people cannot view the screen.

STANDARD 1.07(m)

Social workers should take precautions to ensure and maintain the confidentiality of information transmitted to other parties through the use of computers, electronic mail, facsimile machines, telephones and telephone answering

*machines, and other electronic or computer technology. Disclosure of identifying
information should be avoided whenever possible.*

Technological developments have made it possible for social workers to transmit
confidential information quickly and efficiently via various electronic media. Along with
this convenience and efficiency come considerable risks, primarily involving the inappropriate disclosure of confidential information. For example, social workers who use
the Internet for professional purposes need to be careful to protect clients' privacy and
confidentiality. Practitioners who plan to use the Internet to communicate confidential
or other sensitive information should first obtain clients' informed consent and inform
clients about the potential risks involved (such as security breaches).

Similarly, social workers should be aware of several risks associated with the use
of fax machines. The confidentiality of faxed communications can be breached in several ways. The receiving fax machine may not be in a secure location (out in the open in
an administrative assistant's office, for example); unauthorized parties thus may have
access to faxed confidential communications. In addition, the receiving fax machine's
telephone number could be misdialed inadvertently, sending the confidential communication to an inappropriate destination.

Social workers should avoid sending confidential information via fax machine.
When faxing confidential information seems necessary (as in an emergency), social
workers should notify the recipient by telephone that a fax is being sent and obtain the
recipient's agreement to go to the fax machine immediately to await the document's
arrival. Ideally, social workers should obtain clients' informed consent authorizing them
to convey information via fax. Further, the cover sheet should include a statement to
alert recipients to the confidential nature of the communication, along with the sender's
telephone number, for example,

> The documents accompanying this fax transmission may contain confidential informa-
> tion. The information is intended for the use of only the individual(s) or entity(ies)
> named above. If you are not the intended recipient, you are advised that any disclosure,
> copying, distribution, or the taking of any action based on the contents of this informa-
> tion is prohibited. If you have received this fax in error, please notify us immediately by
> telephone at the above number to arrange for return of the documents.

Telephones and telephone answering devices also can be problematic. Social workers should not discuss confidential information on portable or landline telephones in
locations where their conversations can be overheard. Social workers also should be
careful not to include confidential information in a message on a telephone answering
device or voicemail when it is possible that the message could be heard by a third party
(for example, another member of a client's household or an office mate of a colleague
for whom a social worker leaves a message). In fact, social workers should discuss with
clients what kind of information should be left on the clients' telephone answering
devices. In one case a social worker in private practice left a detailed message on a client's
voicemail, including information about where to seek additional help related to the
client's substance abuse problem. The client's partner was unaware of the client's problem until she listened to the social worker's message before the client arrived home. In
another case a social worker employed in a public child welfare agency left a detailed

message concerning a client on a colleague's home telephone voicemail; the colleague was under contract with the public child welfare agency to provide clinical services to the child in the agency's custody. The colleague's spouse arrived home first that evening and listened to the message, which contained considerable confidential information.

STANDARD 1.07(n)

Social workers should transfer or dispose of clients' records in a manner that protects clients' confidentiality and is consistent with state statutes governing records and social work licensure.

Social workers who transfer a case record to another practitioner should take steps to ensure that unauthorized individuals do not have access to confidential information. Delivery services should be selected based on their ability to protect the confidentiality of the information.

Social workers should dispose of records, when appropriate (see Standard 3.04[d]), in a manner that protects client confidentiality. Records should be shredded or otherwise destroyed so that unauthorized individuals cannot gain access to confidential information. In one case, an agency disposed of old client files by placing them, unshredded, in the trash. The trash hauler had a collision with an automobile on the way to the local dump and portions of case records were strewn over the highway.

STANDARD 1.07(o)

Social workers should take reasonable precautions to protect client confidentiality in the event of the social worker's termination of practice, incapacitation, or death.

Social workers need to anticipate the possibility that at some point they may not be able to continue working with clients because of illness, disability, incapacitation, or death. To ensure continuity of service and to protect clients' confidential records, social workers should make arrangements with colleagues to assume at least initial responsibility for their cases in the event they are unable to continue practicing. This may take the form of oral or written agreements with colleagues or stipulations that appear in a plan the social worker develops with the assistance of a lawyer (for example, designating a personal representative who will handle the social worker's professional affairs). Many experts recommend that social workers prepare a will that includes plans for the transfer or disposition of cases in the event of the practitioner's death or incapacitation. The will can provide for an executor or trustee who will maintain records for a certain period (30 days, for example), at the end of which the social worker's practice and all records will be sold to a designated colleague (typically for a nominal fee). A major advantage of such arrangements is that they limit unauthorized persons' access to confidential information.

Social workers who expect to retire or move to another community should give clients as much notice as possible and make arrangements to respond to telephone calls or other inquiries from clients (such as arranging for a colleague to respond). Social workers who plan to refer clients to other providers should always give clients several names to avoid the appearance that they are actively "steering" clients. Selected colleagues, supervisors, and administrators should be acquainted with details concerning the handling of the social worker's affairs in the event that he or she terminates practice or becomes unavailable.

In one case, a social worker in private practice in a rural community died without having made any arrangements for a colleague to step in and handle clients' matters. Several of the social worker's clients were in crisis at the time of the death and did not know where to turn for assistance. In desperation, a member of the social worker's family looked through the clients' files to provide them with help, thereby breaching the clients' confidentiality.

STANDARD 1.07(p)

Social workers should not disclose identifying information when discussing clients for teaching or training purposes unless the client has consented to disclosure of confidential information.

Social work educators and trainers often use case material to illustrate conceptual points, a widely used and respected pedagogical approach in all professions. When presenting case material in classroom or agency settings or at professional workshops or conferences, social workers must be careful to protect clients' confidentiality—identifying information should not be disclosed without clients' informed consent. Social workers who present case illustrations during a lecture, class discussion, workshop, or conference presentation should not mention clients' names and should disguise or alter case-related details to ensure that the audience cannot identify the clients or other individuals involved. One common strategy is to change details concerning clients' gender, age, ethnicity, race, religion, clinical history, geographic setting, and family circumstances in a way that does not detract from the educational or training point or interfere with the educator's or trainer's goal. Any written case material that a social work educator or trainer distributes should be similarly disguised.

Sometimes social work educators or trainers present videotaped or audiotaped material, especially taped clinical sessions. Such material should not be presented unless clients have provided informed consent to the taping itself (see Standard 1.03 [f]) and to the presentation of the tape to an audience. With videotapes, it may be possible to protect client confidentiality by taping clients from an angle that limits their visibility or using technological devices to blur distinguishing characteristics or disguise voices, but in some instances (group or family therapy, for example), this may be difficult.

Social workers who seek clients' informed consent to disclose identifying information during teaching or training must use their best judgment as to the clients' ability and competence to make a sound decision. Clients who are asked for their consent may be vulnerable for clinical or other reasons; they may feel pressured to provide their consent to the disclosure when it is not in their best interest to do so. Social workers must be careful not to exploit clients or take advantage of their vulnerability.

Social work educators' responsibility also extends to their students. That is, social work educators who arrange for or encourage students' presentation of case material must inform the students about their obligation to protect client confidentiality. Social work educators should discuss with their students methods they can use to disguise case material and avoid disclosing identifying information without client consent.

STANDARD 1.07(q)

Social workers should not disclose identifying information when discussing clients with consultants unless the client has consented to disclosure of confidential information or there is a compelling need for such disclosure.

Social workers encounter many situations in which consultation with colleagues may be helpful or necessary. A social worker who specializes in the treatment of eating disorders may be working with a client who has a serious substance abuse problem. She may want to consult with a colleague with expertise in the treatment of substance abuse problems to discuss how these issues might be addressed effectively within the context of treatment for an eating disorder. A social worker in a nursing home who is providing services to an elderly client who has clinical depression may want to consult with a psychiatrist about effective treatment approaches.

Two important confidentiality issues can arise during consultation. First, clients routinely should be informed, ideally at the beginning of treatment, that social workers sometimes find it useful or necessary to consult with colleagues to provide the most effective services possible. Clients have the right to know that this is how a professional social worker functions. Second, whenever possible, social workers who find it necessary to disclose identifying information to a consultant should obtain clients' informed consent in advance. This may not always be possible, particularly in a crisis or emergency, but every effort should be made to obtain a client's consent before disclosing any identifying or other confidential information.

Social workers often can obtain consultation without disclosing identifying information. To provide useful feedback and advice, consultants may need to know only basic, nonidentifying demographic and clinical information. Social workers can often obtain valuable consultation without disclosing clients' names and by limiting their description of clients to clinically relevant details of clients' age, ethnicity, religion, family circumstances, clinical issues, and so forth. Identifying information should not be disclosed unless there is a compelling reason to do so (see Standard 2.05[c]). There are times, however, when consultants would be able to provide more useful feedback or advice if they were to know clients' names, particularly when the consultant has had prior contact with the client. Ordinarily, social workers should obtain clients' consent before disclosing such identifying information to consultants, but exceptions may be necessary during a genuine crisis or emergency.

STANDARD 1.07(r)

Social workers should protect the confidentiality of deceased clients consistent with the preceding standards.

Social workers sometimes receive requests for confidential information about former clients who have died. Surviving family members of a client who has committed suicide may ask for information to help them cope with their loss, or social workers may be subpoenaed in a legal case involving a dispute among family members concerning the former client's will. A reporter or law enforcement official may request information about a deceased client who was the victim of a serious crime, or an Internal Revenue Service agent may seek information about a deceased client's lifestyle.

Social workers must be diligent in their efforts to protect the confidentiality of deceased clients. They should not disclose confidential information unless they have received proper legal authorization to do so (for example, from the legal representative of the client's estate or by a court order). Disclosure of confidential information without such authorization would constitute a violation of the former client's confidentiality rights.

In a highly publicized case, a clinical social worker was approached by a reporter after a client's death. She made the mistake of disclosing confidential information to the reporter and was subsequently sanctioned by her state licensing board. As part of the sanction, the social worker was required to write a comprehensive guide on confidentiality issues in social work and mail it to all licensed social workers in the state where she practiced. The preface to the guide included the following statement (some details have been altered to protect the social worker's privacy):

> I am a clinical social worker in private practice specializing in treating people with substance abuse problems. Most of my 15 years of experience has been in substance abuse treatment programs. I serve a large suburban area of about 70,000 people.
> Two years ago I thought confidentiality ended at death and spoke to news reporters about a dramatic incident involving a case. I soon realized that this had breached the confidentiality of a client. This booklet is written as part of a sanction for that ethical misconduct.

Social workers who receive requests for confidential information about deceased clients may need to seek legal advice before disclosing any information. When disclosure of confidential information has been authorized or is considered appropriate, practitioners should disclose the least amount of information necessary to achieve the purposes of the disclosure (see Standards 1.07[c] and 2.05[c]).

Access to Records

STANDARD 1.08(a)

Social workers should provide clients with reasonable access to records concerning the clients. Social workers who are concerned that clients' access to their records could cause serious misunderstanding or harm to the client should provide assistance in interpreting the records and consultation with the client regarding the records. Social workers should limit clients' access to their records, or portions of their records, only in exceptional circumstances when there is compelling evidence that such access would cause serious harm to the client. Both clients' requests and the rationale for withholding some or all of the record should be documented in clients' files.

On occasion clients ask their social workers if they can see copies of their clinical record. Clients may be curious about the language or terms their social workers have used to describe their situations or symptoms, or they may be concerned about how other individuals or agencies that have access to the records (an estranged spouse, courts of law, or insurance providers, for instance) might interpret entries in the records.

- A 38-year-old man, a social worker, sought counseling from another social worker to help him deal with what he described as "overwhelming anxiety." With the exception of a small copayment, the counseling was paid for by the client's health insurance provider. The client was concerned that a colleague of his who worked for the health insurance provider approving mental health benefits would see some of the paper work in his case. The client asked the therapist to let him see the case record.
- A 42-year-old woman was referred to a social worker by the court, which had placed the woman on probation after her third arrest for shoplifting. The judge expected a progress report from the social worker at the conclusion of counseling. After five weeks of counseling, the client asked the social worker whether she could read his clinical notes.
- The parents of an 11-year-old boy with serious behavioral issues arranged for their son to receive counseling from a social worker. According to the parents, the boy had suddenly become "very hard to manage" and was "beginning to hang out with a tough crowd." The parents said they were concerned that their son was starting to experiment with drugs. After two months of counseling, the parents informed the social worker that they would like to see a copy of the record.
- A 51-year-old man sought counseling from a social worker to help him cope with bitter divorce proceedings. The man learned from his estranged spouse that she was planning to seek sole custody of their children. The man worried that the social worker's clinical notes—which included details about the man's suicidal ideation and substance abuse problems—might be used against him in the custody dispute. The man told the social worker that he would like to see the social worker's clinical notes.

As a general rule, social workers are obligated to provide clients with reasonable access to their records. Practitioners have come to recognize that clients have a right to know what social workers record about their life circumstances, mental health symptoms, treatment plans, and progress. Earlier in the profession's history, relatively few social workers believed that clients should have the right to examine their own records, and records were typically viewed as agency property. More recently, this thinking has evolved: Social workers now understand why clients may want or need to see their records and that such disclosure can be therapeutically beneficial if handled properly. Shortly before the ratification of the 1979 *NASW Code of Ethics,* Wilson (1978) noted,

> Only a few short years ago, the social work profession simply assumed that a record was the private property of the professional or the agency, and that was that. A few therapists occasionally advocated client participation in recording as part of the therapeutic process, and others began using the video-recorded interview as a means of allowing the individual to study how he communicates and to provide feedback regarding the therapist's effectiveness. However, such procedures were considered experimental rather than routine. . . . There will be increasing pressure from consumers (and also as a result of the ethical philosophy of the social work profession) for all settings to be more open in sharing record materials with clients. (pp. 83, 85)

At times social workers may be concerned that clients' access to their records could be harmful or cause serious misunderstanding. This may occur because, in the social worker's judgment, the client is too fragile emotionally to handle reading the social worker's notes about the clinical situation, or the client is likely to misunderstand what the social worker has written. With few exceptions, even in these circumstances social workers have an obligation to provide clients with access to their records. When practitioners are concerned that access could be harmful or lead to some misunderstanding, they should talk with the client about the records' content and help him or her interpret the records. Only in the most extreme circumstances—when there is compelling evidence that a client's access to the records would cause serious harm—should social workers withhold records (or portions of records). This could occur, for example, when a social worker has evidence that a client is suicidal or homicidal and that providing the client with access to specific information in the case record would likely lead to serious harm. In such exceptional circumstances, both the client's request to see the record and the social worker's rationale for withholding some or all of it should be documented. Consultation with colleagues, supervisors, and legal counsel may be important in these situations, because there is widespread presumption that clients should have access to their records. Clients who are denied access to their records may have grounds for a lawsuit or ethics complaint.

Social workers should explore whether relevant regulations or statutes permit them to use professional discretion in deciding whether to provide clients with access to case records. For example, the federal Freedom of Information Act (1996) and similar laws in all states provide for client access to records maintained by the government, including public social work agencies. According to Saltzman and Proch (1990), "These laws usually allow people to obtain any records maintained by a public agency, whether or not they relate to them, unless access to one's own records would be harmful or access to records which relate to others is precluded by a confidentiality law" (p. 409).

Social workers should always explore clients' reasons for requesting access to their records. The reasons for these requests vary; clients simply may be curious about the social worker's perceptions and opinions, or they may be unhappy about the quality of some aspect of the treatment and want information that can be used against the social worker or agency in a negligence lawsuit. Social workers routinely should inform clients of the emotional risk that can be associated with reading material in their records.

In one case, a clinical social worker for a family services agency provided crisis intervention services to a woman who was depressed because of work-related problems. The client, who had been referred to the social worker through her company's EAP, said she was depressed because she faced racial discrimination at work. The social worker met with the client four times to help her address her symptoms and discuss various longer-term treatment options.

After the third session, the client contacted the social worker and asked to see his case notes. The client explained that she was suing her employer for racial discrimination she had experienced and wanted to give her lawyer a copy of the notes. The social worker was concerned that some of the entries would confuse or upset the client and told her that he had retained only the demographic information required by the EAP. The client ultimately filed an ethics complaint against the social worker, and the social worker was sanctioned for not providing his client with reasonable access to the clinical record. The social worker might have prevented the ethics complaint had he reviewed the *NASW Code of Ethics* and consulted with colleagues about the client's initial request.

Social workers who provide services to minor children need to be particularly careful to respond appropriately when parents or legal guardians request access to a child's clinical record. Many social workers explain to their minor clients and to their parents or guardians that the case record will be considered confidential, subject to the customary exceptions (for example, when a case record is subpoenaed during legal proceedings or there is a court order mandating disclosure of all or parts of a case record). This explanation often suffices and discourages parents and guardians from requesting access to the case record. Occasions may arise, however, when a parent or guardian insists on having access to the case record. In the absence of a local statute governing parents' and guardians' access to confidential information about their children, many lawyers argue that parents and guardians have a legal right to confidential information. That is, parents or guardians who have legal custody have a legal right to inspect case records pertaining to their children unless there is compelling evidence that the children would be at risk of serious harm or the child is considered under the law to be a mature or emancipated minor. As Saltzman and Proch (1990) concluded, "Generally parents are entitled to their children's records if the children would be entitled to the records themselves if they were adults. Records related to birth control, treatment for substance abuse, or treatment for venereal disease are generally excepted from this rule, however" (p. 409). Social workers should keep in mind that details they include in case records about children may be seen by their parents or guardians; the obligation to document the issues addressed and the services provided to children must be balanced with the obligation to protect children's privacy.

STANDARD 1.08(b)

When providing clients with access to their records, social workers should take steps to protect the confidentiality of other individuals identified or discussed in such records.

It is not unusual for case records to contain confidential information about third parties. Whenever clients request access to their records, social workers should review the records to ensure that information shared with the client does not violate other individuals' right to confidentiality. This includes information in the case records obtained from third parties, for example, other service providers or clients' relatives. Confidential information about third parties should not be shared with clients unless the third parties have consented to such disclosure.

In one case, a clinical social worker provided marriage counseling to a couple. With the clients' consent, the social worker occasionally met individually with each spouse. The social worker's case notes summarized both the marriage counseling and the individual counseling sessions.

Eventually the husband decided to seek counseling elsewhere. The husband's new counselor asked for a copy of the first social worker's case notes, which contained confidential references to the wife. The social worker obtained the wife's consent before forwarding a copy of the notes to the new practitioner. At the wife's request—and consistent with Standard 1.08(b)—the social worker withheld several details in the case notes, specifically concerning the wife, that the wife did not feel comfortable disclosing to the new practitioner.

Sexual Relationships

STANDARD 1.09(a)

Social workers should under no circumstances engage in sexual activities or sexual contact with current clients, whether such contact is consensual or forced.

As discussed in the section on dual and multiple relationships, social workers must be vigilant in their efforts to maintain clear boundaries in their relationships with clients. This includes avoiding any sexual activities or contact with current clients. Any form of sexual activity or contact with clients is generally considered self-serving and exploitative regardless of the social worker's motives. Clients who become sexually involved with their social workers are likely to be confused about the nature and purposes of the relationship, and this is likely to be detrimental to them.

- A social worker at a neighborhood health center provided counseling to a woman who was being treated for a serious kidney ailment. The social worker and the client met weekly for about six weeks. The client often talked about how alone she felt and how eager she was for companionship. The social worker, who was attracted to his client, asked her if she would like to have dinner with him later in the week. The client accepted the invitation. Within three weeks, the social worker and the woman, who continued to be the social worker's client, began a sexual relationship.
- A social worker in private practice provided counseling to a man whose marriage was ending. After several months, the social worker—whose own marriage was in trouble—found herself fantasizing about having an affair with her client. Within two weeks the social worker and the client became sexually involved. At the ethics committee hearing, the social worker and the client claimed that the client was not harmed by this consensual relationship.
- A school social worker provided counseling to a 17-year-old student who was having difficulty in her relationship with her parents. According to the social worker, he "gave into temptation when the student began behaving seductively." "I know what I did was wrong," he said. "At the time I managed to convince myself that this student was unusually mature and could handle this sort of relationship."

Allegations of sexual misconduct are among the most common made by clients who file ethics complaints against social workers (Reamer, 1997b, 2003b). These complaints often allege that a social worker and client had sexual contact during the course of the professional–client relationship. On occasion social workers who have had complaints filed against them have argued that the sexual contact was a consensual and legitimate form of therapeutic intervention—that is, the social worker claims to have attempted, with the client's consent, to "help the client address intimacy issues" or "accept the fact that she is lovable." An alternative argument has been put forth by several practitioners that the sexual relationship was conducted independently of the professional–client relationship, that the social worker and client were able to distinguish between their sexual and professional relationships. Neither argument is credible. Social workers have an obligation to avoid sexual contact with clients whether such contact is consensual or forced.

STANDARD 1.09(b)

Social workers should not engage in sexual activities or sexual contact with clients' relatives or other individuals with whom clients maintain a close personal relationship when there is a risk of exploitation or potential harm to the client. Sexual activity or sexual contact with clients' relatives or other individuals with whom clients maintain a personal relationship has the potential to be harmful to the client and may make it difficult for the social worker and client to maintain appropriate professional boundaries. Social workers—not their clients, their clients' relatives, or other individuals with whom the client maintains a personal relationship—assume the full burden for setting clear, appropriate, and culturally sensitive boundaries.

A social worker's sexual relationships with a client's relative or another person to whom the client is close may cause the client to feel betrayed and can undermine confidence in the social worker and the social work profession. Social workers are obligated primarily to protect clients' interests (see Standard 1.01) and must avoid conflicts of interest that may be harmful to clients (see Standards 1.06[a] and [b]).

In some cases, social workers' relationships with clients' relatives or other individuals with whom clients have a close personal relationship are clearly inappropriate:

- A school social worker provided counseling to an 11-year-old student who was referred by a teacher. The student was having difficulty establishing and maintaining friendships and asked his teacher for help. After meeting with the student, the social worker arranged to meet with the student's mother, a single parent. During the course of the social worker's professional relationship with the student, the social worker began a sexual affair with the student's mother that continued after the termination of the social worker's professional relationship with the student.
- A social worker for a home health care agency provided casework services to an elderly woman who was recovering from heart surgery. During one of the home visits, the social worker met the client's adult son. Several weeks later, the client's son contacted the social worker and invited her to join him for dinner and a play. The social worker accepted the invitation, and the two began dating regularly and then began a sexual relationship. The social worker continued to provide professional services to the elderly woman during the course of her relationship with the client's son.
- A social worker in a community mental health setting provided counseling to a 27-year-old woman who was having difficulty in her relationship with her parents. About eight weeks after the professional–client relationship began, the social worker happened to meet the client's sister at a party in the community. Eventually the social worker and the client's sister began a sexual relationship, which began while the social worker was providing services to the woman's sister.

In each of these examples it is easy to imagine how the client might feel betrayed by the social worker's sexual relationship with the client's relative and how this relationship could interfere with the social worker's effectiveness. In other cases, however, social workers may disagree about whether a sexual relationship with a client's relative or other individual to whom a client is close is inappropriate. Below are examples that may generate disagreement among practitioners:

- A social worker employed by a state prison provided occasional counseling to an inmate serving a three-year sentence for assault with a deadly weapon. The social worker happened to meet the inmate's second cousin at a friend's party. The social worker and the inmate's cousin began dating and considered beginning a sexual relationship. The social worker learned from the inmate that he and his cousin had not had contact with each other in seven years and had no plans to resume contact.
- A social worker in a vocational training program provided supportive services to a 22-year-old man with a mental disability. The client participated in a sheltered workshop and had contact with the social worker every other week. The social worker also met occasionally with the client's parents. At a holiday dinner the social worker met a woman who was a "good friend" of the client's mother. The social worker and the woman began to date and planned to enter into a sexual relationship.

When social workers disagree or are unsure about the appropriateness of a sexual relationship with a client's relative or an individual to whom a client is close, it must be clear that the social worker assumes the full burden and considerable risk should he or she decide to enter into such a relationship. When faced with uncertainty, social workers who are considering entering into such a relationship should consult with knowledgeable colleagues and supervisors. Social workers who find themselves in ambiguous circumstances should be as concerned about the possible appearance of impropriety as impropriety itself.

STANDARD 1.09(c)

Social workers should not engage in sexual activities or sexual contact with former clients because of the potential for harm to the client. If social workers engage in conduct contrary to this prohibition or claim that an exception to this prohibition is warranted because of extraordinary circumstances, it is social workers—not their clients—who assume the full burden of demonstrating that the former client has not been exploited, coerced, or manipulated, intentionally or unintentionally.

The general presumption in social work is that practitioners should not enter into sexual relationships with former clients. First, it is not unusual for former clients to face challenging issues in their lives after the formal termination of the professional–client relationship. New emotional issues, relationship problems, or developmental crises, for example, may emerge, and former clients may find it useful to contact the social worker for assistance. The social worker's familiarity with the client's circumstances and the established relationship between the social worker and client may be especially helpful in such cases; "starting from scratch" with a new provider may be both inefficient and intimidating. Clearly, however, a social worker and former client who have entered into a sexual relationship could have difficulty resuming an effective professional–client relationship. Social workers and former clients who enter into sexual relationships after the termination of their professional–client relationship essentially forfeit resuming that relationship, and this may not be in the client's best interest.

Second, former clients may encounter less challenging new issues or problems in their lives and still may find it helpful to speculate about what their former social worker would have said about the matter. The former client may not feel the need to resume a formal relationship with the social worker; however, the client might find it helpful merely to reflect on the social worker's perspective. A sexual relationship between the social worker and the former client presumably would interfere with the former client's ability to draw on what he or she has learned from the social worker's professional expertise, given the shift from a professional to an intimate relationship. Thus, social workers should consider their clients as "clients in perpetuity": once a client, always a client.

In some exceptional circumstances, a sexual relationship with a former client may be permissible because of unusual and extraordinary circumstances:

- A social worker who earned a living as a researcher and program evaluator had a contract to evaluate a home-based, family intervention program. The social worker's primary contact at the agency was the executive director. Five years after the evaluation was completed, the social worker and the agency executive director happened to encounter each other at the home of a mutual friend. They discovered that each was "available" and decided to go out on a date; eventually they engaged in a sexual relationship. In their judgment a sexual relationship was not inappropriate because of the nonclinical nature of their original professional–client relationship and the amount of time that had passed since they had worked together.
- A hospital social worker had two relatively brief conversations with a patient who was being treated for a serious orthopedic problem. The social worker helped the patient arrange home-based health care to begin after discharge from the hospital. The social worker and patient spent a total of 30 minutes together during the patient's hospital stay and exclusively discussed logistical details of the discharge plan. About three years after the patient's hospital discharge, the social worker and former patient met each other at a swim club to which both belonged. They began dating and eventually began a sexual relationship. The social worker concluded that the sexual relationship was permissible because of the brief nature of their professional–client relationship and the fact that their professional–client relationship was concerned with discharge planning issues and not emotional or psychotherapeutic issues.

There is virtual consensus in the social work profession that practitioners involved in clinical relationships with clients (providing counseling or psychotherapeutic services) should not enter into sexual relationships with those clients after termination of the professional–client relationship. In some extraordinary circumstances, a sexual relationship with a former client may be permissible, but social workers who reach such a conclusion should be aware that they assume the full burden of demonstrating that the former client has not been exploited, coerced, or manipulated, intentionally or unintentionally.

Social workers who believe that an exception to this prohibition may be warranted should take several important factors into consideration (Reamer, 2001c):

- How much time has passed since termination of the professional–client relationship? Clearly, a sexual relationship that begins shortly after termination is more suspect than one that begins long after the social worker's services to the client have ended. This question is difficult to answer because there is no magical length of time that must elapse so that a sexual relationship can be "appropriate."
- To what extent is the client mentally competent and emotionally stable? A sexual relationship with a former client who has a lengthy history of emotional instability and vulnerability is a greater cause for concern than a relationship with a former client who is clearly competent and emotionally stable.
- What issues were addressed in the professional–client relationship? A sexual relationship after a professional–client relationship that involved discussion or examination of emotionally sensitive and intimate issues is more problematic than a relationship limited to such activities as program evaluation, fundraising, and political action.
- How long did the professional–client relationship last? Should a sexual relationship develop, a professional–client relationship that lasted for many months is a greater cause for concern than a relationship that lasted for 30 minutes.
- What circumstances surrounded the termination of the professional–client relationship? Was it terminated so that the social worker and the client could begin a sexual relationship, or did it come to a natural conclusion because the requisite work was done? The social worker must carefully examine the motives and circumstances surrounding the termination of the professional–client relationship (see Standard 1.16[d]).
- To what extent is there foreseeable harm to the client or others as a result of a sexual relationship? How likely is it that the client could be harmed by a sexual relationship, especially if that relationship ends unpleasantly? Could those who are close to the client—such as a spouse or partner—be harmed by a social worker's sexual relationship with the client? To what extent could the client's ability to trust social workers be harmed by the relationship? Is it likely that rumors about the relationship would undermine the profession's integrity?

Certainly these are difficult questions to answer. Social workers may answer them differently based on their particular education and training, professional experience, and personal philosophy. In the final analysis, social workers must recognize that there is a general proscription against sexual involvement with any former client and that, should they decide that exceptional circumstances justify a sexual relationship with a former client, social workers assume the full burden of responsibility.

STANDARD 1.09(d)

Social workers should not provide clinical services to individuals with whom they have had a prior sexual relationship. Providing clinical services to a former sexual partner has the potential to be harmful to the individual and is likely to make it difficult for the social worker and individual to maintain appropriate professional boundaries.

Obviously, social workers have personal lives that may involve sexual relationships. Ideally, such relationships involve mutually intimate sharings of information and feelings. In its purest form, an intimate relationship between two people is not hierarchical in nature, with one person assuming more authority, power, or control than the other.

Moving from an intimate sexual relationship to a professional–client relationship can be detrimental to the client. Former lovers who become clients may find it difficult to shift from the role of an egalitarian partner in a relationship to a party who, to some degree, is in a dependent or subordinate position. No matter how much a social worker believes in empowering clients and engaging clients as equal partners in the helping relationship, clients are, by definition, in the position of someone asking for or required to receive assistance (a form of dependency), and the social worker is in the position of authority charged with providing assistance. This inescapable dynamic places clients in a vulnerable position that reflects the power imbalance in the relationship.

Confusion about the nature of the relationship could cause a client who was sexually involved with a social worker before the onset of the professional–client relationship to be unable to benefit fully from the social worker's expertise. The client may have difficulty distinguishing between the social worker's professional and personal roles in his or her life. The couple's interpersonal history and dynamics may interfere with the client's ability to receive help and the social worker's ability to provide help. The social worker's influence and credibility might be undermined because of the client's intimate familiarity with the social worker's personal life and issues.

In psychodynamic terms, the transference and countertransference involved in such a relationship are likely to limit the social worker's effectiveness and the ability of both client and practitioner to maintain appropriate professional boundaries. *Transference* is a frequent phenomenon in psychotherapy: A client's emotional reactions in the current relationship with the social worker may be stimulated or triggered by former experiences, relationships, or developmental conflicts in his or her life. Given the possibility of transference, a client's feelings about and reactions to a social worker may be complicated by emotional experiences in the sexual relationship with the social worker that preceded the professional–client relationship. In *countertransference,* a social worker's emotional reactions to a client may have originated in the social worker's own prior experiences, relationships, or developmental conflicts (Barker, 2003). In this context, the practitioner's feelings about and reactions to the client may be affected by the intimate relationship with the client that occurred before the professional–client relationship.

For example, a social worker in private practice was contacted by a former lover about 18 months after the end of their intimate relationship. The couple had been sexually involved for a little more than a year and had ended the relationship amicably. They had agreed to remain friends and had had sporadic contact since. The former lover told the social worker that he "really needed to talk to someone about some issues" and she was "the person who knows me best and the person I trust the most." After seeing the social worker professionally for eight sessions, the client discovered that he had strong, unresolved, romantic feelings for the social worker, and these feelings were distracting. The client felt that he had not accomplished very much in his therapy and his confusion about his relationship with the social worker was hindering his progress. The client shared this realization with the social worker, who acknowledged that she, too, was finding the client–professional relationship difficult to manage. "In retrospect," the social worker told her client, "I shouldn't have agreed to be your therapist. That was a mistake." Consistent with Standard 1.09(d) (see also Standard 1.16[a]), the social worker recommended that the client see another therapist for assistance.

Physical Contact

STANDARD 1.10

Social workers should not engage in physical contact with clients when there is a possibility of psychological harm to the client as a result of the contact (such as cradling or caressing clients). Social workers who engage in appropriate physical contact with clients are responsible for setting clear, appropriate, and culturally sensitive boundaries that govern such physical contact.

Social workers must always be careful to distinguish between appropriate and inappropriate physical contact with clients. Appropriate physical contact may take various forms—its essential feature is that it is not likely to cause clients psychological harm:

- A social worker was employed by a residential program for children with serious emotional and behavioral problems. One of the residents was an 11-year-old boy who often engaged in self-destructive behaviors. He had been severely abused by his father. One day a police officer informed the social worker that the boy's mother, to whom he was very attached emotionally, had died of a drug overdose. The social worker broke the news to the boy, who was distraught and cried uncontrollably. The social worker sat down beside the boy, put her arm around him, and rested her head against his as he sobbed.
- A social worker for a home health care agency provided services to a 42-year-old woman who was dying of breast cancer and leukemia. The social worker sat at the patient's bedside and listened while she talked about the end of her life and her concern about how her husband and young children would handle her death. The woman cried intermittently as she talked about her grief and speculated about her family's uncertain future. The patient held out her hand for the social worker to hold. The social worker held and stroked the patient's hand and arm as they talked.
- A social worker at a family services agency provided counseling to a college student who was struggling with self-esteem issues. The counseling lasted for four months. According to the client, the counseling was enormously helpful, and she was deeply grateful for the social worker's insight and skill. The client reported that her "entire world view had changed as a result of this intense experience." At the end of the last session the client thanked the social worker and initiated a good-bye hug that lasted about three seconds.

In these three situations the social workers had brief and limited physical contact that is generally considered acceptable. None of these clients would likely be psychologically harmed by the contact. To the contrary, most likely they would find the physical contact psychologically comforting, as a form of consolation or "therapeutic touch."

In contrast to these situations are those involving physical touch that has more potential to cause clients psychological harm. In general, inappropriate physical touch occurs when the nature of the touch might exacerbate the client's transference in harmful ways, thus confusing or troubling the client; or perhaps the touch might suggest that the relationship between the social worker and client extends beyond the formal professional–client relationship. For example,

- A social worker in private practice provided counseling to a young woman who reported being depressed ever since acknowledging that, as a young child and teenager, she had been sexually abused by her stepfather. The social worker and client focused mostly on the client's self-esteem issues and her difficulty sustaining intimate relationships with men. Toward the end of one particular counseling session, which took place about 10 months after the start of the therapy, the client began to cry about the trauma she had endured. The social worker got up from his chair and sat next to the client on the sofa to comfort her, and he put his arms around the client while she leaned against him. He held her tight, rocking her back and forth while she cried. The social worker continued to hold and stroke the client after her crying had subsided.
- A social worker in private practice specialized in providing group therapy to women who had been physically and sexually abused. As a routine part of therapy, the social worker asked group members to sit in a circle on the floor ("to get down low, on the same level, and as a way to get in touch with the small child within themselves," the social worker said), then she lowered the office lights and turned on soothing music. In the course of this part of the therapy, each client had an opportunity to experience being nurtured by the social worker: the social worker sat on the floor with her legs spread open, and the client sat with her back against the social worker's chest and the social worker's arms wrapped around her. The social worker rocked the client and spoke soothingly and softly to the client's "inner hurt child." At times, the social worker would wipe away the client's tears and gently stroke her hair. The social worker said this provided clients with "a corrective emotional experience" and "constructive reparenting."
- A clinical social worker had a long-standing interest in the therapeutic effects of massage. She had not received formal training as a massage therapist but had learned a number of massage techniques from a close friend. The social worker was providing counseling to a recently divorced 52-year-old woman. The client explained that she had divorced her husband after realizing that she was a lesbian and had sought counseling to address her difficulty coping with the dissolution of her marriage and the dramatic changes in her life. During a session the client commented that in recent weeks she had been feeling unusually "tense and tight," a reflection of the anxiety she had been experiencing. The social worker suggested that some massage might be helpful and offered to rub the client's shoulders, neck, head, face, arms, and back during their therapy session.

These situations can be problematic because the social worker's conduct has the potential to confuse clients about the nature of the professional–client relationship and introduce complex boundary issues into the relationship. Some forms of touch—especially cradling and caressing, which typically have a sexual connotation—are likely to distract both social workers and clients from their therapeutic agenda and thus jeopardize the client's well-being. Other than brief contact for therapeutic purposes—such as a quick hug to say good-bye or to console a distraught client—physical touch is likely to cause psychological harm and interfere with the professional–client relationship.

Sexual Harassment

STANDARD 1.11

Social workers should not sexually harass clients. Sexual harassment includes sexual advances, sexual solicitation, requests for sexual favors, and other verbal or physical conduct of a sexual nature.

Not only is social workers' sexual contact with clients unethical, sexual harassment in any form is unethical as well. According to Conte (2000), sexual harassment can take three forms: verbal (pressure for sexual activity, comments about a person's body, sexual boasting, and sexist or homophobic comments), nonverbal (suggestive looks or sounds or obscene gestures), and physical (touching, patting, pinching, kissing, and rape).

Sexual harassment of clients can be psychologically harmful. It can cause emotional stress and trauma, guilt, and shame. As Singer (1995) noted,

> these afflictions result from the double bind of abuse—giving in to the abuse to avoid penalty and facing the indignities or fighting the abuse with the resultant threat of retaliation. Some victims report symptoms characteristic of those with posttraumatic stress disorder—that is, recurring nightmares, nonspecific fears, and anger years after the event. (p. 2152)

In addition to its impact on clients, sexual harassment also can undermine the social work profession's integrity and credibility with the public:

- A social worker employed by a women's prison provided individual and group counseling to inmates. He met regularly with one inmate who was serving a three-year sentence for possession and distribution of drugs. During one of the counseling sessions, the social worker told the inmate that she had a "great figure."
- A clinical social worker in private practice provided counseling to a 32-year-old woman who was separated from her husband. The client sought counseling to address several issues related to the end of the marriage. The client's managed health care company refused to authorize more than six counseling sessions. Toward the end of the fifth session, the client said she felt the need for more counseling but did not have the funds to pay for it. The social worker, who felt attracted to the client, suggested that they "might be able to work something out" and asked the client whether she would be interested in spending "some time with me away from the office, just the two of us."
- A social worker in the military provided counseling to an 18-year-old soldier. The soldier reported feeling depressed because he was away from his home and family for the first time. At the conclusion of the second counseling session, the social worker patted the soldier on the buttocks as he was leaving his office.

Social workers are obligated to avoid any behaviors that constitute sexual harassment. They should not make sexual advances toward clients, solicit sexual favors, or make comments or gestures of a sexual nature.

Derogatory Language

STANDARD 1.12

Social workers should not use derogatory language in their written or verbal communications to or about clients. Social workers should use accurate and respectful language in all communications to and about clients.

Social workers must be careful to avoid disparaging or pejorative language in their comments to or about clients simply because it is disrespectful. Below is an excerpt with inappropriate language from a case record in a child protective services agency; the entry was written by a social work student who was completing a field placement in the agency (details have been altered to protect the client's privacy):

> I visited the Smith home to investigate allegations of child neglect. I was met at the door by Mrs. Smith, a single parent. I was surprised by her size; she was morbidly obese and smelled as if she hadn't showered in weeks. Rolls of fat hung out of Mrs. Smith's shirt, and portions of her legs were covered with dirt. Mrs. Smith's slovenly appearance suggests that she is unable to care for herself, much less her children.

In addition to being disrespectful, certain forms of derogatory language can expose social workers to legal risk, as when there is evidence of defamation of character. Defamation occurs as a result of "the publication of anything injurious to the good name or reputation of another, or which tends to bring him into disrepute" (Gifis, 1991, p. 124). It can take two forms: libel and slander. *Libel* occurs when the publication is in written form—for example, in a social worker's progress report about a client that is read by a judge or employer concerned with the client's circumstances. *Slander* occurs when the publication is in oral form—for example, when a social worker testifies about a client in a court of law or provides an oral report about the client's progress to a probation officer.

Social workers can be legally liable for defamation of character if they say or write something about a client that is untrue, if they knew or should have known that the statement was untrue, and if the communication caused some injury to the client (for instance, the client was terminated from a social services program or fired from a job). In one case a hospital social worker referred to a newborn infant as a "cocaine baby" because of a number of symptoms manifested by the baby at birth. Based in part on the social worker's assessment and report, the baby was placed in foster care against the mother's wishes. Subsequent laboratory tests confirmed that, although the baby manifested symptoms similar to those found in infants delivered by mothers who had used cocaine, in this particular case the baby suffered from a syndrome unrelated to cocaine use. The mother ultimately filed a lawsuit alleging defamation of character against the hospital and the social worker. As a result of this experience, the social worker learned that he must characterize clients very carefully, avoiding any terms or labels that might not be true or accurate. In this case, for example, the social worker might have written at the time of the birth: "Baby seems agitated; Dr. X suspects baby may be experiencing withdrawal symptoms from mother's drug use; awaiting results of toxicology screen."

In another case a social worker in a child welfare agency was responsible for screening prospective foster parents. As part of the process of screening prospective foster parents for licensing, the social worker conducted personal interviews with applicants, ran criminal background checks, and contacted personal references. The social worker rejected an applicant's request to be a foster parent after reviewing his criminal record. According to the case notes, the applicant had been convicted two years earlier of assault with a deadly weapon; the incident apparently arose from a violent argument between the applicant and a neighbor. Based on this information, the social worker concluded that the applicant would not be a fit foster parent.

The applicant sued the social worker for defamation of character (among other claims related to the rejection of his application). He was able to demonstrate that, in fact, he had not been convicted of assault with a deadly weapon, as reported by the social worker. Rather, the criminal charges had been dismissed. The social worker had misinterpreted the documents he examined and concluded, wrongly, that the applicant had been convicted of the offense when he had only been charged with the offense.

In a case that took place in a major hospital, a social worker provided assistance to the parents of a child who had been rushed to the emergency department after a serious accident. At the time the child's mother was distraught and argued with hospital staff about being allowed access to her son, who died in the emergency department. According to the social worker's case notes, the mother suffered from "pre-morbid separation issues which will complicate bereavement," was involved in a "shaky marriage," and was "narcissistic." The mother filed a lawsuit against the social worker alleging defamation of character.

The best way for social workers to prevent defamation of character claims is to report information about clients accurately. The best defense against such an allegation is that the written or oral statement was true (Madden, 2003; Stein, 2004).

Payment for Services

STANDARD 1.13(a)

When setting fees, social workers should ensure that the fees are fair, reasonable, and commensurate with the services performed. Consideration should be given to clients' ability to pay.

Many factors are considered in social workers' determination of professional fees. Practitioners typically are influenced greatly by the marketplace—the fees charged by other professionals for comparable services. As a result, most private practitioners charge clients an hourly rate similar to that charged by colleagues with comparable education in that geographic area. Per diem rates for such services as residential treatment and day treatment programs tend to be similar, if not identical, within geographic areas; agencies in locations with a higher cost of living may charge higher fees. Similarly, fees charged by agencies for services such as adoption home studies, geriatric assessments, and clinical evaluations are usually influenced by market forces. Social workers, like most other professionals, usually want to be in line with the industry standard, so they do not price themselves out of the market or earn substantially less than their colleagues.

Other factors also influence social workers' fees. As part of a managed care program, insurance providers may negotiate specific reimbursement rates with social workers for mental health and other social services. Some social workers set their fees above the field's norms to influence the kinds of people who seek their services; social workers who charge fees above the norm may do so to limit their clientele to affluent clients who can afford to pay all or part of the fee out of pocket. Other social workers may set their fees below the field's norms so that access to services will be enhanced, particularly for low-income people.

On occasion ethical questions are raised about social workers' fees. For example, a couple interested in adopting a child consulted with a family services agency that had just started to provide adoption services (for example, conducting home studies, facilitating placements, providing pre- and post-adoption counseling). The agency director, a social worker, knew that prospective adoptive parents often feel desperate and are willing to pay large sums of money to adopt an infant. The agency director told the assistant director that by setting high fees, the agency—the only one in the area providing adoption services—had a "golden opportunity to generate substantial revenue." The assistant director told the agency director that she felt this would be exploitative and unethical.

Standard 1.13(a) explicitly encourages social workers to take clients' ability to pay into account when they set fees. Historically, the social work profession has been concerned about the well-being of low-income people. The preamble to the *NASW Code of Ethics* asserts, "The primary mission of the social work profession is to enhance human well-being and help meet basic human needs of all people, with particular attention to the needs and empowerment of people who are vulnerable, oppressed, and living in poverty" (p. 1). To the extent possible, then, social workers should make their services available to people of little or modest means. Of course, this is more feasible in some cases than in others. Some social workers and agencies are not in a financial position to reduce their fees or otherwise underwrite the costs associated with delivering services. Thus, the code does not require social workers to set fees based on clients' ability to pay; rather, it exhorts social workers to be sensitive to clients' ability to pay. According to the code's summary of ethical principles, "Social workers are encouraged to volunteer some portion of their professional skills with no expectation of significant financial return (pro bono service)" (p. 5).

STANDARD 1.13(b)

Social workers should avoid accepting goods or services from clients as payment for professional services. Bartering arrangements, particularly involving services, create the potential for conflicts of interest, exploitation, and inappropriate boundaries in social workers' relationships with clients. Social workers should explore and may participate in bartering only in very limited circumstances when it can be demonstrated that such arrangements are an accepted practice among professionals in the local community, considered to be essential for the provision of services, negotiated without coercion, and entered into at the client's initiative and with the client's informed consent. Social workers who accept goods or services from clients as payment for professional services assume the full burden of demonstrating that this arrangement will not be detrimental to the client or the professional relationship.

The majority of clients (or their insurance providers) pay fees for social services, but in a relatively few cases, social workers participate in barter arrangements when clients are unable to pay for services and offer goods or services as a substitute. Bartering also occurs in some communities in which there are established norms involving such nonmonetary exchange of goods and services.

On the surface, barter may not seem to pose ethical problems if the parties participate willingly. In actuality, though, barter may lead to troubling ethical questions, as in this example:

A social worker in private practice provided counseling services to a young man who manifested symptoms of mild depression. In general, the client functioned well in the community; he was involved in a long-term relationship and earned his living as a house painter. With the social worker's help, the client began exploring a number of family issues that seemed to be related to his depression.

The client's managed care provider authorized six counseling sessions. The company was not willing to authorize additional sessions, despite the social worker's detailed explanation of the client's wish for additional assistance. To be helpful to the client, the social worker, whose office badly needed painting, suggested that they work out an arrangement by which the client would paint the social worker's office in exchange for counseling services. The client agreed to the proposal and, after some initial disagreement about the fair market value of the paint job, the two determined the number of counseling sessions that would be traded for it (fair market value for the paint job divided by the social worker's customary hourly fee).

Shortly after the painting was completed, while the client was still in counseling with the social worker, a wall in the social worker's office began to peel. She brought this to the client's attention, but the client said it would be some time before he could repair the wall because he had other commitments. The two also disagreed about the cause of the peeling. The social worker was concerned about the appearance of her office and began to lose patience with the client. She ultimately admitted that her feelings about the client's handling of the defective paint job affected her professional relationship with him.

This case illustrates what can be ethically problematic in barter arrangements. Negotiations about the fair market value of the goods or services to be exchanged and, in particular, about the handling of defects in a product or service can interfere with the social worker–client clinical relationship in a way that is harmful to the client. In addition, the services the social worker provides to the client may be determined by the market value of the goods or services provided by the client rather than the client's clinical needs. Especially because the client may be dependent on the social worker, and because of the unequal power relationship between the parties, the client may be vulnerable to exploitation, conflicts of interest, or coercion.

Some social workers argue, however, that barter is ethical, particularly in communities where it is an accepted practice (for example, where farmers commonly exchange hay or corn for plumbing or carpentry services). In light of this argument, the NASW Code of Ethics Revision Committee concluded that it would not be appropriate categorically to prohibit barter arrangements between social workers and clients. Rather, the committee took the position that social workers should avoid bartering and that they should accept goods or services from clients as payment for professional services only in very limited circumstances when certain conditions are met. First, to what extent are such arrangements an accepted practice among professionals in the local community? The widespread use of barter in the local community can strengthen a social worker's contention that this was an appropriate practice in a particular case. Second, to what extent is barter essential for the provision of services? Is it used merely because it is the most expedient and convenient form of payment available, or is it used because it is the only reasonable way for the client to obtain needed services? As a general rule, barter should be considered as a last resort only when more conventional forms of payment have been ruled out and only when it is essential for the provision of services. Third, is the barter arrangement negotiated without coercion? Social workers should not pressure clients to agree to barter. For example, feeling some coercion, a client may agree reluctantly to give a social worker a treasured work of art from the client's personal collection, primarily because the social worker has commented on how much he or she would like to own such a work. Clients who agree to participate in a barter arrangement must do so freely and willingly, without any direct or indirect coercion from the social worker. Fourth, was the barter arrangement entered into at the client's initiative and with the client's informed consent? To avoid coercing clients or the appearance of such impropriety, social workers should not take the initiative to suggest barter as an option. Such suggestions should come from clients, with their fully informed consent. Social workers should explain the nature and terms of the arrangement in clear and understandable language and discuss risks associated with barter (for example, how the professional–client relationship could be adversely affected, particularly if there is a defect in the goods or services provided by the client in exchange for the social worker's services), reasonable alternatives for payment (for example, a reduced monthly payment rather than payment in full or by credit card), the client's right to refuse or withdraw consent, and the time frame covered by the consent (see Standard 1.03[a]).

Social workers must recognize that even when all these conditions have been met, they assume the full burden of demonstrating that bartering will not be detrimental to the client or the professional relationship. Their principal responsibility is to protect clients: Practitioners must exercise sound judgment when considering the risks associated with barter.

STANDARD 1.13(c)

Social workers should not solicit a private fee or other remuneration for providing services to clients who are entitled to such available services through the social workers' employer or agency.

Many social workers provide services in more than one setting. They may have two or more part-time jobs, for example, or a practitioner who is employed full-time in a social services agency also may have a part-time private practice. Social workers who provide services in more than one setting must maintain clear boundaries between the settings, particularly with respect to payment for services.

In one case, a social worker was employed as a caseworker in a public child welfare agency. His responsibilities included supervising children in foster care and providing counseling to parents who were trying to regain custody of children who had been abused or neglected. In addition to his full-time position, the social worker maintained a part-time private practice.

In his position at the child welfare agency, the social worker provided casework and counseling services to a family whose eight-year-old child was in foster care; the child had been placed in foster care after he was physically abused by his father. In the social worker's judgment, the family would benefit from more counseling than he could provide in his position at the child welfare agency. He shared his views with the family and offered to see them in his private practice. The family agreed, and paid him a reduced out-of-pocket fee.

This arrangement is unethical because there was a conflict of interest. The social worker stood to benefit personally from seeing the clients in his private practice. He did not attempt to arrange for the child welfare agency to provide more in-depth counseling under its own auspices; rather, he essentially referred his clients to himself. To avoid this conflict, the social worker should have conferred with supervisors or administrators at the child welfare agency to arrange for additional counseling services for the family to be provided by staff of the child welfare agency or by another professional in their local community.

Clients Who Lack Decision-Making Capacity

STANDARD 1.14

When social workers act on behalf of clients who lack the capacity to make informed decisions, social workers should take reasonable steps to safeguard the interests and rights of those clients.

Social workers sometimes provide services to clients who lack the capacity to make informed decisions as a result of, for example, a brain injury, mental illness or disability, or a drug overdose. Ordinarily, a person is deemed incompetent when, because of age, mental illness, mental disability, excessive use of drugs or alcohol, or some other form of mental or physical incapacity, he or she is incapable of either managing his or her property or caring for himself or herself (Dickson, 1995; Madden, 2003; Stein, 2004).

To protect such clients, social workers should be knowledgeable about their legal rights. In general, adults in the United States are presumed to be legally competent and entitled to make all decisions for themselves. They can be deprived of this right only if they have been determined to be incompetent by a court that considers evidence concerning mental or physical impairment. It is possible that a person is considered to have a mental illness, a developmental disability, or alcoholism, for example, but competent to make decisions, manage money, and care for himself or herself; that is, impairment or disability does not, by itself, imply incompetence (Madden, 2003; Stein, 2004). As Saltzman and Proch (1990) asserted, the presumption of competency

should only be overcome if a person is incapable of making certain or all decisions and it is necessary to have another make the decisions to protect the incapable person. The presumption should not be overcome merely because a person might make unwise decisions or decisions that could cause harm to himself or herself. Adults have a right to be wrong. The state may intervene to protect a person incapable of making a rational decision on a certain matter or any rational decisions under the doctrine of parens patriae, but . . . the breadth and vagueness of the definition of incompetence in many statutes, as well as the lack of procedural protections in guardianship proceedings, may result in findings of incompetence that are not justified. (pp. 329–330)

Social workers who provide services to clients who lack the capacity to make informed decisions should be knowledgeable about these clients' legal rights in a number of key areas. As discussed under Standard 1.03(c), social workers should protect clients' interests by seeking informed consent on a client's behalf, when necessary, from an appropriate third party (proxy or substituted judgment). This person is usually a spouse, partner, or other relative who is likely to act in the client's best interests or who has been appointed as the client's legal guardian. To the extent possible, a social worker should explain to such a client, in a manner consistent with the client's level of understanding, what services are being provided, what options are available, and what decisions are being made. This may not be possible with some clients (for example, clients with profound mental disability or serious brain injury), but it is possible with many (for example, certain clients with moderate mental disability or who are recovering from a serious drug overdose).

Social workers also should be aware that many states now require that judicial decisions concerning an individual's incompetence should focus narrowly on specific issues or circumstances rather than take the form of a broad determination that an individual is incompetent for any and all purposes. Thus, a client may be considered incompetent to make sound decisions about handling a large inheritance yet competent to make a decision about where to live. A court might then appoint a guardian to handle only the client's financial matters; the guardian would not have the authority to determine where the client will live. Many states recognize the concept of "least-restrictive alternative" as a guiding principle, which states that a person considered incompetent should lose only those rights that he or she cannot properly exercise (Dickson, 1995; Stein, 2004).

In these situations, a number of important issues arise with respect to health care decisions. Generally speaking, competent adults have a right to refuse medical treatment. When an individual is incompetent, a court may appoint a legal guardian to make a decision on that individual's behalf. A court also may use a substituted judgment test by which it attempts to determine what the client would want. This subjective test contrasts with an objective test by which the court attempts to determine what a reasonable person would want. Some courts have recognized an incompetent individual's prior expression of wishes and desires concerning medical treatment, even when such wishes and desires were not documented in writing, as in a living will (Dickson, 1995; Madden, 2003).

Although in most cases minor children are not considered competent to consent to their own medical treatment, exceptions do exist. In many states minor children are permitted to consent to medical treatment in cases of genuine emergency or if they want assistance with birth control or treatment for substance abuse or a sexually transmitted disease.

Social workers in mental health settings should be familiar with laws and regulations concerning clients' right to treatment, right to refuse treatment, and right to humane treatment in the least-restrictive manner (particularly with respect to religious freedom, freedom of speech, privacy and visitation rights, the right to be free of restraints and seclusion, and the right to personal property). With the exception of certain rights that are federally protected such as civil rights and the right to privacy, the rights of incompetent individuals and related laws and regulations can vary from jurisdiction to jurisdiction. Agencies would be wise to develop written guidelines and policies that reflect local laws and regulations.

Interruption of Services

STANDARD 1.15

Social workers should make reasonable efforts to ensure continuity of services in the event that services are interrupted by factors such as unavailability, relocation, illness, disability, or death.

Social workers' services to clients are sometimes interrupted, expectedly or unexpectedly. For example, a social worker may have to leave town—suddenly and temporarily—to care for an ill parent, or may move to a new city or state for professional or personal reasons. A social worker could also be unavailable because of a planned vacation, retirement, a sudden illness, disability, or death.

Social workers should anticipate the possibility that they may not be available to clients who are in need of assistance and arrange for adequate coverage. Different circumstances require different contingency plans. Social workers who know ahead of time that they will be unavailable because of vacation or personal leave (for planned surgery or maternity leave, for example) should arrange for a colleague to provide coverage. The colleague should be selected carefully, to ensure that the individual who will provide coverage has the requisite education and expertise to assist one's clients. For example, a social worker in private practice who specializes in services to elderly clients should arrange for a colleague with comparable expertise to provide coverage, not a colleague who specializes in treatment of adolescent substance abusers.

As discussed above with respect to Standard 1.07(o), social workers who know that they will be leaving a work setting for another position, retiring, or moving away also should take steps to ensure continuity of services. When leaving an agency for another work setting, a practitioner should be sure that a qualified colleague in the former workplace will assume responsibility for his or her clients. The social worker should spend time in conference with the colleague to ensure that he or she has sufficient information to meet clients' needs. Of course, social workers should inform clients of their plans as soon as possible (ideally at least several months in advance) and make clear that the clients have the option to obtain services elsewhere. Similarly, social workers who are retiring should inform clients as soon as possible and discuss referral possibilities. Social workers in private practice who plan to move out of the geographic area should help active clients select another services provider and inform clients of their new location, in case the clients or other authorized parties need to have access to information in case records.

Because illness, disability, and death are unpredictable, social workers also should identify colleagues who will provide coverage in the event that they are suddenly and unexpectedly unavailable. Social workers in private practice should consider consulting with a lawyer to develop a plan that names a personal representative authorized to handle client matters, referrals to new services providers, and client records.

Ethical problems can arise when social workers are not available when they are needed by clients. In one case, a social worker in part-time private practice left town suddenly to care for a disabled relative. He did not arrange back-up coverage until one week after his departure. Before coverage was arranged, however, one of his clients became suicidal and attempted to contact the social worker for assistance. After several failed attempts to reach the social worker, the client jumped from a highway overpass and killed himself.

In another case, an independent social worker died suddenly after a heart attack. She had not contacted a lawyer to plan for the appointment of a personal representative and had not consulted a colleague about providing emergency coverage. Several of the social worker's clients became distraught when they discovered that she had died and had left no contingency plan.

Termination of Services

STANDARD 1.16(a)

Social workers should terminate services to clients and professional relationships with them when such services and relationships are no longer required or no longer serve the clients' needs or interests.

Social workers use a variety of criteria and data to determine when it is appropriate to terminate services to clients and professional relationships with them. In some circumstances, social workers and clients may agree in advance to work together for a specific length of time. For example, clinical social workers and their clients may contract for a specific number of counseling sessions, or a social worker retained as an organizational consultant may have a contract to work on a project for a specified period of time. This may occur at the initiative of the social worker, the client, or some third party, for example, an insurance or managed care company that authorizes a specific number of sessions.

In other circumstances social workers terminate services when clients reach specific goals. For example, a client may wish to continue seeing a social worker until a divorce is finalized or until a child's behavior shows marked improvement, or social work consultants may provide services until certain project goals are reached.

Some social workers provide services to clients in a relatively open-ended fashion. Certain clients who want counseling may not feel comfortable agreeing to a specific number of sessions; they may prefer to see where the sessions go and what they achieve, making decisions along the way about the length of service. A social worker who is a community organizer may not have a structured time frame in work with residents of a particular neighborhood, preferring instead to follow the community's lead (assuming there is ample funding to support the activities).

No matter how social workers approach the delivery of services, whether closed- or open-ended, they must terminate services to clients and professional relationships with them when such services and relationships are no longer required or no longer serve the clients' needs or interests (that is, if the services were not terminated because of the client's uncooperativeness or lack of compliance with program requirements, or because of a client's failure to pay for services). If, in the social worker's judgment, a client has accomplished what he or she has set out to achieve, the social worker has a responsibility to talk with the client about terminating the professional–client relationship.

Ethical issues arise when social workers do not terminate services to and relationships with clients even though the services are no longer needed or no longer serve the clients' needs and interests. This most often occurs for one of two reasons. First, social workers who are particularly concerned about their income may discourage clients from terminating or fail to broach the subject of termination because they wish to maintain the revenue that these clients provide. In one case, an independent social worker provided counseling to an affluent man who reported struggling with a midlife crisis. The client was considering abandoning his lucrative business career to pursue an uncertain career as an artist. After the 13th clinical session the social worker believed that the client had adequately addressed the clinical issues. However, the social worker, who had a number of serious financial concerns, was worried about losing the income generated by this self-paying client. As a result, he was much more assertive than usual in his effort to have the client identify other issues in his life that might require counseling. The social worker soon realized that, for self-interested reasons, he was trying much too hard to hold on to the client.

Second, to meet their own emotional needs, social workers may extend services beyond what is clinically appropriate or necessary. A social worker may find working with a particular client to be unusually satisfying and rewarding or may, unconsciously perhaps, want to encourage the client's dependency. In the case discussed above of the client who was contemplating a career change, the social worker discovered that working with the client was also helping him explore his own ambivalence about a possible career change. Through his work with the client, the social worker achieved a number of useful insights into his own goals and circumstances.

Social workers need to be careful not to place their own interests above those of their clients. As one of the code's ethical principles states, "social workers elevate service to others above self-interest" (p. 5). Social workers must be sure not to let the financial and emotional rewards associated with their work guide their decisions about termination of services to clients and professional relationships with them.

STANDARD 1.16(b)

Social workers should take reasonable steps to avoid abandoning clients who are still in need of services. Social workers should withdraw services precipitously only under unusual circumstances, giving careful consideration to all factors in the situation and taking care to minimize possible adverse effects. Social workers should assist in making appropriate arrangements for continuation of services when necessary.

Social workers need to be concerned about terminating services prematurely and not being available when a client needs assistance. On occasion, practitioners terminate services to clients who are not making adequate progress; whose behavior toward the social worker is hostile, resistant, or uncooperative; who have needs that require services outside the social worker's areas of expertise; who threaten a social worker's safety or file a complaint or lawsuit against him or her; who do not comply with a treatment plan or provisions of a contract; who have exhausted their insurance coverage; or who do not pay an overdue balance (see Standard 1.16[c]).

In one case, an ethics complaint was filed against a social worker at a community mental health agency by a former client who alleged that the social worker had terminated services abruptly. The client, who had a severe disability, had sought counseling to help her develop skills to cope with her chronic impairment. After several months of intervention, the social worker began having difficulty working with the client. According to the social worker, the client was "demanding, resistant, and aggressive." She reported that the client telephoned her incessantly, often leaving angry messages concerning the social worker's lack of responsiveness.

During one intense exchange with the client, the social worker became irritated and told the client that she "would be much better off with another counselor." The social worker terminated services shortly thereafter. The client sent the social worker a registered letter asking for a detailed explanation of her decision to terminate services, but the social worker refused to accept the letter. In addition, the social worker made no attempt to provide the client with names of other practitioners whom she could contact for assistance. Although the social worker's frustration in this case may be understandable, she clearly violated ethical standards by not terminating services properly.

Social workers who terminate services to clients who are still in need of assistance or who are not available when needed (for example, when they go on vacation or resign their job) risk allegations of abandonment. *Abandonment* is a legal concept that pertains to instances when a professional is not available to a client when needed (Madden, 2003; Reamer, 2003b). Once a social worker begins to provide services to a client, she or he incurs a legal responsibility to continue those services or properly to refer a client to an alternative services provider (see Standards 2.06[a] and [b]).

Social workers should take several steps to avoid abandoning clients (Austin et al., 1990; Reamer, 2003b; Schutz, 1982):

- Consult with colleagues and supervisors about a decision to terminate services. In some cases, termination can be prevented by addressing relevant issues. For example, social workers may be able to address a client's reason for not paying an overdue balance and develop a workable payment plan. Social workers whose clients are not making reasonable progress may be able to modify their intervention to enhance the clients' progress.
- Give as much advance warning as possible to clients who will be terminated.
- Provide clients with the names, addresses, and telephone numbers of at least three appropriate referrals when it is necessary to terminate services.
- When clients announce their decision to terminate prematurely, explain to them the risks involved and offer suggestions for alternative services. Include this information in a follow-up letter.
- In cases involving discharge of clients from a residential facility, be sure that a comprehensive discharge plan has been formulated and significant others have been

notified of the client's discharge (clients should be informed of this). In cases involving court-ordered clients, seek legal consultation and court approval before terminating care.

- Follow up with a client who has been terminated. If she or he does not go to the referral, write a letter to the client about the risks involved should she or he not follow through with the referral.
- Provide clients with clear instructions to follow and telephone numbers to use in case of emergency. Include a copy of these instructions in their case records. Ask clients to sign this copy, indicating that they received the instructions and the instructions were explained to them.
- When away from the office for an extended time, call in regularly for messages. Social workers who are away from the office should leave an emergency telephone number with an administrative assistant, an answering service, or an answering device. Social workers who anticipate that certain clients may need assistance during their absence should refer those clients to a colleague with appropriate expertise.
- Carefully document in the case record all decisions and actions related to termination of services.

STANDARD 1.16(c)

Social workers in fee-for-service settings may terminate services to clients who are not paying an overdue balance if the financial contractual arrangements have been made clear to the client, if the client does not pose an imminent danger to self or others, and if the clinical and other consequences of the current nonpayment have been addressed and discussed with the client.

Some clients are unwilling or unable to pay an overdue balance for professional services rendered by a social worker. Social workers should first discuss with such clients the reasons for nonpayment and take reasonable steps to help clients meet their financial obligations without terminating services. For example, if a client does not pay her overdue balance because she is angry or upset about some aspect of the services received, the social worker should discuss that dissatisfaction with her and attempt to address her concerns. If a client does not pay his overdue balance because of sudden unemployment, the social worker should consider trying to work out a reasonable payment plan, which might include reducing the fee to an affordable level.

If attempts to address a client's reasons for nonpayment of an overdue balance fail, the social worker may terminate services, but only when two conditions have been met. First, the social worker should be confident that the client does not pose a danger to himself or herself or others. It would be unethical to terminate services to an actively suicidal or homicidal client, even though the client has an unpaid balance.

Second, a social worker who is considering terminating services should first discuss with the client the possible clinical and other consequences of the nonpayment and termination of services. What clinical risks would the client face if he or she stopped receiving services? What emotional and psychological implications might there be? How might family members and other friends and acquaintances be affected by the termination of services? Social workers should document their impressions in the case record, which can help ensure that these issues are addressed with clients and protect social workers, should questions later be raised about the decision to terminate services.

In one case, a social worker in private practice provided counseling services to a young woman who was distraught after the break-up of a long-term relationship. Under the terms of the client's insurance coverage, she was responsible for a 50 percent co-payment for each counseling session. After three months, she had accumulated a very large outstanding balance. The social worker terminated services, and the client filed an ethics complaint and a lawsuit alleging that the social worker terminated services inappropriately. The social worker was unable to provide documentation indicating that she had discussed with the client how the nonpayment might be addressed or the possible clinical implications of the nonpayment. Also, the social worker was vulnerable because she had allowed the client to accrue such a large outstanding balance, one that the social worker knew the client was not likely to be able to pay off.

In another case, a social worker provided clinical services to a client who had been diagnosed with dysthymia (an affective disorder involving symptoms of depression). The client reported to the social worker that occasionally he had fleeting thoughts about committing suicide. The social worker assessed the client for suicide risk by use of a standardized suicide assessment protocol, and he concluded that the client did not pose an imminent risk of suicide. Eventually the social worker terminated services to the client because the client had not paid his large overdue balance. Two weeks after the termination of services, the client attempted unsuccessfully to commit suicide; as a result of the attempt he suffered grave physical injuries (brain injury due to loss of blood). The client filed a lawsuit and an ethics complaint against the social worker, alleging that he had terminated services without properly assessing the client's suicide risk. At issue was the timing of the suicide assessment that the social worker had conducted and on which he based his judgment; the client claimed that the suicide assessment was conducted at the beginning of the professional–client relationship and was out of date by the time the social worker decided to terminate services. The social worker was vulnerable because he did not have documentation in the case file confirming that he had properly assessed for suicide risk at the time services to the client were terminated.

STANDARD 1.16(d)

Social workers should not terminate services to pursue a social, financial, or sexual relationship with a client.

During the course of their work with clients, social workers may be tempted to become involved with clients socially, financially, or sexually. The code of ethics proscribes dual and multiple relationships (Standard 1.06[c]), and such relationships are not permissible even if the professional–client relationship has been terminated. However, some social workers may be tempted to terminate a professional–client relationship to pursue a social, financial, or sexual relationship, as in these examples:

- A social worker for a family services agency provided individual counseling to a woman, a single mother, who wanted advice about managing her son's behavioral problems. The social worker provided counseling services to the mother and, on occasion, her son over a period of three months. During the third month, the social worker and the mother acknowledged that they were attracted to each other. Knowing that an intimate relationship with a client is prohibited by the code of ethics, the social worker referred the client to a colleague for further counseling, terminated the professional–client relationship, and began dating her shortly thereafter.

- A social worker in private practice provided counseling to a man who was having difficulty coping with some problems at work. After working together for some time, the client told the social worker that he was planning to start his own business to get away from his problems at work. The client told the social worker about his plans to start a restaurant supply business (a field in which he had considerable expertise and experience) and how he needed to raise capital to get the business off the ground. The client asked the social worker if he would like to become a financial partner in the new business. The social worker found the investment opportunity appealing and talked to his client about how they would need to terminate their professional–client relationship if they became business partners. The client and social worker agreed to terminate the professional–client relationship and soon thereafter entered into a business relationship.

It is unethical for social workers to terminate a professional–client relationship to pursue a social, financial, or sexual relationship. As in the case of Standard 1.09(c), which concerns sexual involvement with former clients, entering into dual and multiple relationships after the termination of the professional–client relationship can exploit and harm clients. Because of the unequal power in the relationship, clients may be particularly susceptible to social workers' suggestions or influence concerning post-termination social, financial, or sexual relationships. In addition, as discussed elsewhere in this chapter, entering into such a dual or multiple relationship after termination can confuse a client about the social worker's role in his or her life and can interfere with the client's ability and opportunity to draw on the social worker's expertise should issues arise that would warrant professional social work assistance.

STANDARD 1.16(e)

Social workers who anticipate the termination or interruption of services to clients should notify clients promptly and seek the transfer, referral, or continuation of services in relation to the clients' needs and preferences.

There are legitimate and understandable reasons why social workers might terminate services to clients who still need some form of assistance. These include planned retirement, resignation to assume a new position, evidence that clients are not making appropriate progress or cooperating with an intervention plan, lack of expertise to assist clients with specific needs, being threatened or sued by clients, and clients' failure to pay an overdue balance. Social workers who anticipate the termination or interruption of services to clients for such reasons should work with them to develop a plan to address their needs. As discussed in relation to Standard 1.16(b), social workers should take several steps to protect clients:

- Give clients as much advance notice as possible.
- Provide clients with the names, addresses, and telephone numbers of at least three appropriate referrals when it is necessary to terminate services.
- When clients announce their decision to terminate prematurely, explain to them the risks involved and suggestions for alternative services. Include this information in a follow-up letter.
- In cases involving discharge of clients from a residential facility, be sure that a comprehensive discharge plan has been formulated and significant others have been notified of the client's discharge (clients should be informed of this). In cases involving court-ordered clients, seek legal consultation and court approval before terminating care.
- Follow up with a client who has been terminated. If she or he does not go to the referral, write a letter to the client about the risks involved should she or he not follow through with the referral.
- Provide clients with clear instructions to follow and telephone numbers to use in case of emergency. Include a copy of these instructions in their case records. Clients should be asked to sign this copy, indicating that they received the instructions and the instructions were explained to them.
- Carefully document in the case record all decisions and actions related to termination of services.

Here is an example of appropriate termination: A social worker who was the clinical director for a community-based psychiatric program (a group home) provided services during a four-month period to a 46-year-old man who had a dual diagnosis of substance abuse and clinical depression. During his stay in the program, the client had difficulty complying with a number of program rules. On several occasions he had sexual contact with another resident, was found with contraband (unauthorized medications), and failed to attend several mandatory group meetings. The social worker and other staff worked with the client to enhance his compliance with program rules. Despite these efforts, the client repeatedly violated the rules. Eventually the staff decided that they would need to ask the client to leave the program.

The social worker took several steps to meet this client's needs. First, she informed him of the staff's decision to discharge him from the program and of their reasons; she also gave him as much notice of the termination as possible given the circumstances (three weeks). Second, she consulted with the client about other possible services providers and explored several options. The social worker gave the client the names, addresses, and telephone numbers of three appropriate referrals and offered to help the client contact these services providers. Third, she prepared a comprehensive discharge plan and, with the client's consent, notified his wife of the pending discharge. Because the client had been admitted to the program as a condition of probation after an arrest for shoplifting, the social worker sought legal consultation and court approval before terminating services. Once the court had approved the discharge and referral to a new program, she followed up with the client to ensure that he had contacted the new services provider. Because the client did not make immediate contact with the new provider, the social worker wrote him a letter about the risks involved should he not follow through with the referral. The social worker also carefully documented in the case record all decisions and actions related to the discharge from the residential program and the termination of services. Thus, ethical practice also is humane care for the client and may provide the social worker with some protection should the client file an ethics complaint or a lawsuit alleging that the social worker mishandled the termination process.

STANDARD 1.16(f)

Social workers who are leaving an employment setting should inform clients of appropriate options for the continuation of services and of the benefits and risks of the options.

As do all professionals, social workers sometimes leave positions of employment for new opportunities. This may occur for a variety of reasons, such as wanting to pursue a new professional challenge, an increase in responsibilities, a change in client population, increased compensation, or a new group of colleagues. Sometimes social workers leave employment settings for "positive" reasons—for example, to develop new skills and to take on more challenging responsibility—but they may also leave employment settings for "negative" reasons—for example, because of conflict with an administrator or dissatisfaction with the tasks required by the job.

Social workers who leave an employment setting should be sure to terminate with clients properly. As discussed concerning Standard 1.16(b), social workers should take specific steps to avoid abandoning clients (such as giving clients as much advance warning as possible and thoroughly discussing the implications of the impending departure, providing clients with detailed information about their options for continuing to receive services, and documenting in the case record all decisions and actions related to arranging continued services for clients who are in need of assistance).

In this discussion with clients, social workers should review all appropriate options for the continuation of services. Ordinarily there are four options. First, clients may choose to terminate services if they feel their needs have been addressed adequately. Second, they may choose to continue receiving services in the social worker's current agency. In this case the social worker and the client should work together to identify another professional in the agency who would assume responsibility for the client's case. The social worker would then consult with the colleague to ensure a smooth transfer (see Standard 2.06[b]). Third, clients may choose to obtain services from another agency or a private provider. Here, too, the social worker and the client should work together to identify another agency or professional in the community with whom the client can feel comfortable. Again, the social worker would consult with the new provider to ensure a smooth transfer.

A fourth option, when feasible, is for clients to continue working with the current social worker in her or his new employment setting. For example, a social worker at a family services agency provided individual counseling to a woman who was having marital difficulties. After working together for nine weeks, the social worker informed the client that, in two months, she would be leaving the agency and establishing a private practice. The social worker informed the client that she could choose to remain at the family services agency and receive assistance from another staff member or obtain services from another agency or practitioner. The client was reluctant to interrupt the continuity of the counseling, give up her rapport with her current social worker, and establish a relationship with a new practitioner. The social worker then explained to the client that she also could choose to continue working with her as a client in the new private practice.

Social workers who inform clients that they may choose to continue working with them in the new employment setting must be exceedingly careful to ensure that the clients are fully aware that this is merely an option; social workers should not pressure or coerce clients to follow them to their new employment setting. A social worker could stand to benefit if clients choose to follow them to a new employment setting, for example, when clients choose to leave their current agency and continue working with the social worker in a new private practice. Practitioners must avoid the appearance of impropriety and actual conflicts of interest that may harm clients (Standards 1.06[a] and [b]). A social worker's primary goal should be to meet clients' needs (Standard 1.01) and respect clients' right to self-determination (Standard 1.02). They should carefully discuss with the client all available and reasonable options and assess their benefits and risks. Clients who choose to follow their social worker to a new employment setting should do so because continuing to work with that social worker is the best way to meet their needs.

In one case, a social worker at a community mental health center provided counseling to a man with alcoholism who was in recovery. After they had worked together for four months, the social worker informed the client that he had decided to leave the agency and establish a private practice. The social worker was very anxious about the financial risk he was taking because he was trading a secure, predictable income for an uncertain one. He knew that it would take some time for him to establish a sufficient clientele and a steady income. The social worker actively encouraged the client to follow him to his new private practice. He spent considerable time pointing out why it would be best for the client to continue working with him and little time discussing other resources available at the community mental health center and elsewhere in the community. Although there may have been sound clinical reasons for the client to follow the social worker to his new private practice, it was unethical for the social worker to actively encourage the client to pursue this option without thoroughly exploring with him—as objectively as possible and without attempting to steer the client toward his private practice—all available and reasonable options.

3

Ethical Responsibilities to Colleagues

The standards in this section of the code concern social workers' relationships with professional colleagues, particularly other social workers. They concern treating colleagues with respect, handling shared confidential information, interdisciplinary collaboration, disputes involving colleagues, consultation, referral for services, sexual relationships with and sexual harassment of colleagues, impairment and incompetence of colleagues, and unethical conduct of colleagues.

Respect

STANDARD 2.01(a)

Social workers should treat colleagues with respect and should represent accurately and fairly the qualifications, views, and obligations of colleagues.

Social workers often collaborate with colleagues in various ways and settings. Those who work in agency settings frequently collaborate with colleagues within and outside of their agencies. Social workers in private practice collaborate with colleagues employed in other settings. Such collaboration occurs for many reasons, including case consultation, peer supervision, coordination of services, referral for services, agency audits, quality assurance reviews, program evaluations, and inter- and intra-agency task forces.

Most interactions among social workers occur without conflict. As with all human beings, however, conflict sometimes occurs between practitioners during their professional encounters. Social workers may have professional disagreements concerning a joint task—for example, a decision about how best to intervene with a client or whether services to a client should be terminated. Such conflict may result from legitimate differences of opinion. Social workers also may have personality clashes with one another—they simply do not get along. Even social workers who agree ideologically may find that their personal styles clash; one practitioner may be easy-going and a colleague much more intense and assertive. In addition, conflict between social workers can arise for what might be called "political" reasons. Social workers within an agency who are vying for a particularly attractive administrative opening or promotion may become resentful of each other. Practitioners who head competing agencies in a community may find themselves involved in a "turf battle" of sorts.

Recognizing that conflict with colleagues can arise, social workers always should treat them with respect. In particular, social workers should not undermine colleagues or misrepresent colleagues' views or qualifications to gain a competitive edge. Below are several examples of unethical conduct:

- A social worker employed in a family services agency informed his supervisor that he would be leaving the agency to establish a private practice. For some time the social worker and supervisor had not gotten along. The supervisor contacted the social worker's clients to discuss how the family services agency might best continue to meet their needs. In each conversation, the supervisor told the clients that they would receive more competent care from other staff at the agency than from the social worker who was leaving to establish a private practice. The supervisor intimated to each client that the social worker's skill was not up to the agency's standards, which was the reason for his leaving.
- Two social workers for a public welfare agency applied for the open position of assistant department director. Both were eager to be offered the position. One of the social workers sent an anonymous letter to the department director informing the director that, over a two-year period, his colleague had embellished her travel expenses vouchers and overstated the number of overtime hours she had worked. These claims were wildly exaggerated and intended to cast aspersions on the colleague.
- A social work administrator employed in a hospital also served on the board of directors of a local shelter for battered women. The board was in the process of reviewing several ambitious proposals from social workers in the community who wanted to conduct a program evaluation at the shelter. The proposals were submitted in response to a request for proposals (RFPs) issued by the shelter director several months earlier.

  Years earlier, one of the social workers who submitted an RFP had worked with the social work administrator who served on the board of directors. The two had had a great deal of conflict when they worked together at a local psychiatric hospital. At a board meeting to discuss the various proposals, the social work administrator told his colleagues that the applicant who was his former colleague was "remarkably inept and unskilled." The administrator then tried to convince his colleagues that they would be making a big mistake if they awarded the contract to this particular applicant. In fact, the administrator knew little about the applicant's program evaluation skills; he was simply determined to see that his former "nemesis" did not get the program evaluation contract.

Social workers may encounter situations in which it is tempting to misrepresent colleagues' qualifications, views, or professional duties. Ethically, however, social workers are obligated to "take the high road" and always treat colleagues professionally and with respect.

STANDARD 2.01(b)

Social workers should avoid unwarranted negative criticism of colleagues in communications with clients or with other professionals. Unwarranted nega-

tive criticism may include demeaning comments that refer to colleagues' level of competence or to individuals' attributes such as race, ethnicity, national origin, color, sex, sexual orientation, age, marital status, political belief, religion, and mental or physical disability.

It is unrealistic to expect that social workers should never criticize colleagues in their communications with clients or other professionals. In some relatively rare cases, criticism is warranted. For example, a social worker employed by a public child welfare agency was arrested for having sexual contact with one of the agency's clients. The social worker was convicted of first-degree sexual molestation and sentenced to 18 years in prison. At a meeting of senior staff at the child welfare agency, several social workers spoke critically of their colleague. Although they understood that their colleague's conduct might be explained by serious psychological impairment, the social workers were upset that their colleague would engage in such unconscionable behavior. They were particularly angry because of the damage caused by their colleague to their agency's reputation. Their criticism was legitimate.

In another case, a social work administrator who headed a consortium of residential programs for adolescents with emotional disturbances was terminated by the agency's board of directors after their accountant discovered that the administrator had skimmed a substantial amount of agency funds for his own use. As a result of the social worker's misconduct, several large referral sources suspended referrals to the agency, thus forcing the agency to lay off several staff. The social workers at the agency met to discuss the crisis; during the conversation, several social workers criticized the former administrator for his self-serving behavior. Here, too, the negative criticism was warranted.

It is important for social workers to distinguish between warranted and unwarranted negative criticism of colleagues. Criticism may be warranted when a colleague has engaged in egregiously harmful or unethical behavior. It is generally unwarranted when it takes the form of demeaning, gratuitous, inaccurate, discriminatory, or unfair comments about a colleague's competence or about the colleague's personal attributes related to race, ethnicity, national origin, color, gender, sexual orientation, age, marital status, political beliefs, religion, or mental or physical disability. Below are several examples of unwarranted negative criticism:

- A social worker employed at a high school referred one of the school's students to a social worker at a local community mental health center for counseling. A month after making the referral, the social worker in the high school contacted his colleague at the mental health center and asked for an update on the student's progress. The social worker at the mental health center told her colleague that she could not disclose any information about the student without the student's signed release of information, which was required by law. The high school social worker became angry at his colleague and said, "Aw, come on—give me a break! I'm the one who referred [the student]! Who do you think you are, keeping information from me?" At lunch that day with a colleague from the high school, the high school social worker shared the story and said, "Can you believe that kike [a derogatory term for a person of Jewish descent]? Who does she think she is—holier than thou?"
- A social worker in a group practice provided counseling to a woman who had just terminated her professional–client relationship with another social worker. According to

the client, the social worker she had been seeing "wasn't terribly helpful. I never felt as if I was accomplishing much." Several years earlier, the client's new social worker and the social worker she had been seeing for counseling had been lovers; however, the relationship ended bitterly. Even years later, both harbored considerable resentment. After hearing the client's comment about the social worker she had first seen, the new social worker said, "Yeah, I've had several clients over the years who have had problems with her. It's just as well you got out of there. She can be trouble."

- A social worker for a state juvenile correctional facility was a member of a very conservative religion. The religion's adherents were deeply opposed to homosexuality, believing that it was immoral and forbidden by the Bible. One of the social worker's colleagues at the correctional facility was openly gay and walked with a severe limp that was caused by an injury from a serious automobile accident. During a group therapy session run by the social worker, one of the participants made a snide remark about the gay man's disability. The social worker laughed along with the other youths and said, "You know, that could very well be God's way of punishing him for his sinful behavior."

STANDARD 2.01(c)

Social workers should cooperate with social work colleagues and with colleagues of other professions when such cooperation serves the well-being of clients.

Although social workers occasionally may have conflict with colleagues, they must be careful not to let such conflict interfere with their obligation to meet clients' needs (see Standard 1.01). Interpersonal conflict, ideological clashes, and "turf battles" may occur; however, social workers are obligated to ensure that their own personal issues and agendas do not compromise the quality of care they provide to clients. In one case, for example, a social worker in a drug and alcohol treatment program worked with a client who, in addition to having a serious substance abuse problem, was diagnosed with an eating disorder. The social worker needed to refer the client to a professional who had expertise treating eating disorders, particularly someone who had some understanding of the relationship between eating disorders and substance abuse. In this moderately sized community there was only one professional who had this expertise; unfortunately, this was the social worker's former spouse, from whom he was estranged and with whom he had chosen not to have contact. After giving the matter considerable thought, the social worker concluded that his former spouse was the best person for his client to see professionally, so he contacted his former spouse to arrange the referral. He and his former spouse talked openly and candidly about their obligation to separate their personal differences in relation to their obligation to meet the client's needs.

In another case, a social worker for an employee assistance program (EAP) was contacted by a local psychologist, who was interested in receiving referrals from the EAP. The psychologist had expertise that would be a useful resource for the program. However, the psychologist did not know that he had supervised the social worker's closest friend in another agency. The social worker often had heard from her friend that the psychologist was "brilliant with clients but could be difficult as a colleague." Because of her friend's reports, the social worker was initially reluctant to refer to the psychologist, but